The Trust Seeker

When You Have Nowhere to go but Trust

(in a Deeper Love) by Believing and Receiving

By: Angie Gomez

Published by Franklin Publishers

Printed in the United States of America

For permissions, inquiries, or additional copies, contact:

Franklin Publishers

www.franklinpublishers.com

Dedication

This book is dedicated:

To the ones who feel like they've lost too much.

To the ones who wonder if God still hears them.

To the ones ready to walk away—but who stayed just a little longer.

To the ones in the hallway between doors.

To the dreamers who dare to believe again.

To the weary who are about to rise up in glory.

To every person who thought they were forgotten—this is for you.

May your story reveal the fingerprints of a God who writes beauty through brokenness, and purpose through every pause.

Prayer of Commissioning

Father God,

We thank You for every soul who has read these pages. For the hearts You've stirred. For the lies You've silenced. For the new things You are birthing even now.

We ask that You seal every word in truth. Let nothing planted in faith be uprooted by fear. Let every revelation lead to transformation. Let every promise declared become a door unlocked. May Your presence be near, Your voice be clear, and Your love be undeniable.

Commission each reader into their next step. May they serve You with gladness, walk in peace, love without limits, and trust You in everything. Remind them they are not behind. They are not alone. They are not too late.

This is a *new beginning*.

In Jesus' name,

Amen.

Acknowledgments

I owe a great debt to those at Miracle Tuesday and Thursday mornings prayer for your support, extreme patience, and faithful counsel during the time of waiting and writing process.

To those who took the time to be interviewed: Justin Maina, Melody Brittingham, Pastor Tessa Fuller, and everyone else who played a role in writing this book, such as Pastor Jurgen Matthesius, Pastor Leanne Matthesius, Rex Crain, Pastor Jon Heinrichs, and Pastor Becky Heinrichs.

Thank you to everyone in my life. Kim, Cynthia, Heather, Julie and Vanessa; not only are you dear friends, but you are my Sisters in Christ.

Thank you to my friend Erin for sharing your wisdom and talent to write this book on Trusting God, which helped me find a Love I never knew existed. The gift of your book, One Transforming Love and Trusting God with your Love Story, has been a treasure when I was looking for a Love like the one I never knew existed with My Love, James! To my amazing family: Your faith is a rock. I'm humbled to be surrounded by such a great cloud of witnesses and know that your prayers move mountains!

To my first Project Manager, Robert Riddle: You championed this book, and I am especially grateful for your persistence.

To the entire team at Franklin Publishers: I have been moved completely by your truth, and your excellence continually inspires me. I am especially thankful to my current Project Manager, Noah Cohen, for partnering with me to see women set free by the grace and freedom of Jesus Christ. This book would not be the same without your wise guidance and influence.

I thank God for choosing me to be a faithful steward of your love poured out towards others, and doing exceedingly and abundantly more than I could have ever asked or imagined.

Lastly, I am deeply grateful to God for my husband James. You are a daily reminder of God's goodness and faithfulness. Thank you for never settling for. less than His best and for praying this work into existence. God's best is worth fighting for, worth waiting for, and worth praying for.

Table of Contents

Prologue: Renew Your Mind

"Do not conform to the pattern of this world, but be transformed by the renewing of your mind." —Romans 12:2

In a world full of distractions, pressure, and constant noise, it's easy to lose sight of your calling—and even harder to see who you're truly becoming. But you were never meant to live stuck in fear or shaped by the expectations of this world. You were designed for more.

You were *called* to be an Overcomer. A World Changer. A Light Carrier. A Vessel of Power and Purpose. You hold the ability to shift the atmosphere around you—not through your own strength, but by the Word of God released through your tongue, through your worship, and through your willingness to trust Him.

To renew your mind, as Romans 12:2 urges, is to *actively exchange* worldly thinking for God's truth. It's a daily transformation—choosing to align your thoughts with Scripture, seeking God in prayer, and intentionally building a mindset that honors Him. This isn't just about improving your attitude—it's about allowing your very soul to be reshaped into the likeness of Christ. *"Let this mind be in you which was also in Christ Jesus"* (Philippians 2:5).

But many stop at the threshold of new life. We claim the title of "Christian" yet remain spiritually stagnant because we do not discipline our thoughts, nor do we understand how God has designed us. We blame the enemy when often it's our own untrained mind and unhealed heart holding us back. We remain asleep to the spiritual authority within us. *But oh, what we could be if we truly awakened!*

When life doesn't go as planned—when the job falls through, when the relationship ends, when the storm keeps raging—it's easy to wonder, *Is this really what God has for me?* Yet those moments are not the end of your story. They are sacred invitations. Invitations to grow, to trust, and to see with new eyes.

It's like a puzzle. At first glance, the pieces make no sense. Scattered, disconnected. But slowly—patiently—God reveals how they fit. First, in your heart. Then, in your mind. And finally, deep within your soul. Eventually, you'll look back and see: He was forming something beautiful all along.

He will take you to places you never imagined—not because you planned it perfectly, but because He loves you more than you could ever comprehend. This book is a journey into that trust.

We'll talk about what it really means to believe. To follow. To surrender. To persevere when things don't make sense. Because the secret to navigating life's trials is not in striving harder, but in strengthening your spirit—letting Him stand in the center of your life, not on the sidelines.

You can work for money your whole life, gain accolades, and fill your days with productivity, but without God at the center, it will never be enough. He is not impressed by what you possess. What matters is who you become in His presence. The surrendered life. The trusting heart. The soul aligned with divine purpose.

My prayer is that through these stories, you will find encouragement, healing, and a greater awareness of who God is—and who you are because of Him. May each page remind you that you were created on purpose, for a purpose, and nothing is wasted in His hands.

He is sovereign. He is near. And the strength you need? It's already in you.

Non-negotiable Faith

Oh, Trust—that powerful, beautiful thing we often try to avoid, only to discover how essential it truly is. Like the pieces of a puzzle, God wants us to know that He has us exactly where we need to be, even when we can't see the full picture. Against all odds, we are called to trust—by believing and receiving.

We often hope things will simply work out the way we want. And while life doesn't always go according to our plans, I can tell you this as an optimist: living with hope and positivity makes all the difference. Especially in times like these, hopefulness isn't just helpful—it's vital.

This chapter is about staying rooted in faith—even when it's hard. Especially when we hit our limit and feel like we can't go on. That's when we must choose to put on peace like a garment. In Trina's case, that garment was flannel—something comforting, familiar, and warm. Sometimes, trust must be worn the same way: deliberately, daily, like your favorite coat. We need to prioritize trust—not just feel it, but live it. After all, worry is a choice. And you don't have to choose it.

"The Lord is good to those who hope in Him, to the one who seeks Him."
— *Lamentations 3:25*

There's nothing quite like living in the center of God's plan for your life. It's exciting, fulfilling, and meaningful. But when life hits hard—and it will—things feel more difficult when you're confused about where you're going or why you're even on the path. That's why these stories matter. They're meant to shine a light in dark times and remind you that God is present. He's always hoping you'll choose Him, so He can guide you to your destiny. You are His masterpiece.

Let's go back to where Trina started. Many people may relate to her story if you grew up in a church-going home. She came from a religious background that felt safe and familiar. Tradition and structure were deeply woven into her life. And she's grateful for it—her childhood was beautiful, and most would say she was blessed.

But even so, Trina struggled with trust. Deep down, she often felt defeated, uncertain whether it was really possible to trust God enough to overcome the odds. Maybe it was part of God's design for her to be raised by parents who prioritized Him. Maybe that foundation was the first step toward the trust she would eventually learn.

If we could all learn to face life with that kind of trust, we'd begin to understand something important: our problems, pain, and circumstances can all be transformed with the right mindset. The very things that once set us apart or held us back can become the platform for peace and joy in our future.

But here's the key: we can't move forward with the wrong attitude. Until we realign our thinking and approach life differently, we'll keep facing the same battles. Growth only happens when we believe—truly believe—that **the best is yet to come**.

Trust me, this didn't come easily for Trina. It was a struggle. Until she grasped these truths, she found herself stuck—her own strength was getting her nowhere. Because doing the same things with the same mindset will always produce the same results.

This book will share Trina's journey, and the stories of others who understand the power of giving hope. Why? Because there is a real, living hope available to you—one that will empower you to step out in faith and become the person God created you to be... for others.

Let Faith Be Bigger than Your Fear

Faith is the evidence of things not seen, yet hoped for. That truth alone carries weight. It asks us to pause and reflect. Is believing a critical part of this journey? Absolutely. To truly trust God, we must desire it more than anything else. Since nothing surprises Him—and He is greater than any situation we face—it's necessary to surrender every issue, every burden, into His hands.

He is enough. That's what we can believe in.

True surrender is more than a moment—it's an experience. When it's done with the whole heart, it can feel like a flood pouring through the soul. That's how you know you're really letting go. Isaiah 59:19 says that the Lord raises up a standard, and when He does, it becomes a divine line of defense. His work on the cross established that standard—one the enemy cannot overcome.

Imagine a wall strong enough to protect a city from a rising flood. That is what the crucifixion and resurrection of Jesus created—a defense of salvation, a fortress of grace. Now picture letting that flood of love rush into your heart. It may come through God's promises—through scripture you can read and repeat as often as needed. That flood becomes life itself, washing over your soul.

Trina often felt like a boat drifting in rough waters—overwhelmed by daily life and unsure how to stay afloat. But when she fully surrendered, she experienced a shift. She received a push forward. And more than that, she asked for help—and God met her in the middle of the storm.

Gratitude became part of her breakthrough. Thankfulness opened the door to faith. And faith, in turn, revealed God's heart. She began to see Him not just as a Savior, but as her **Vindicator**—one who stands in her defense, who fights for her.

There were things tying Trina up—barriers that felt immovable. For some, it might be a lack of peace, or joy, or stability. For her, it was the belief that she couldn't move forward. She had embraced a lie that said she wasn't enough. What she needed was a rescuer.

And that's exactly who God became.

When she realized she could partner with Him, everything shifted. The mental rope that once held her back was cut loose. She stopped relying on her own strength and started receiving the Spirit of God—the only true source of power and clarity.

Trina learned to share her struggles with the One who adds glory to the story. She invited God into every part of her life. And as she prayed, she asked for the Spirit of God to live within her—to guide her, comfort her, and lead her with wisdom.

He is the Great Counselor, and He promises to teach us everything we need to know—exactly when we need it.

How It All Started

Once upon a time, in a small cottage nestled in the heart of a lush forest, there lived a young girl named Trina. Each night, she climbed into her bunk bed with a heart heavy from fear and uncertainty. For Trina, the bed wasn't just a place to sleep—it had become a battleground. Beneath the covers and in the silence, imaginary monsters waited, feeding off her anxiety.

As she lay awake, a crushing weight of bitterness and anger pressed down on her chest. With every night that passed, the monsters seemed to grow stronger, fueled by her fears. She tried to push them away, but they returned again and again—gnawing at her peace, robbing her rest.

One night, worn out from the struggle, Trina whispered a simple prayer. "God," she said softly, "please help me. I can't do this alone." In that moment, a wave of calm washed over her. A flicker of hope lit up within her heart—small, but unmistakable.

With newfound courage, she began to imagine those monsters disappearing—removing them one by one. And as she did, the bitterness and anger melted away. In their place came peace, clarity, and the realization that she wasn't facing any of this alone. God was there. He always had been.

As her heart opened to Him, Trina sensed a deep change beginning. One morning, she woke up with a verse pressed into her spirit:

"Blessed are those whose ways are blameless, who walk according to the law of the Lord." —Psalm 119:1

From that night on, Trina began to pray boldly. She learned to trust God's guidance and lean into His protection. The fear that once ruled her began to lose its grip. With each step, she discovered that God truly was with her—and with Him beside her, there was always a path forward. No matter how dark it got, peace was possible.

She also discovered something else: we can't allow fear, worry, or doubt to take up residence in our lives. The enemy, like an unwanted guest, will claim a place—even a "bunk bed"—if left unchallenged. But just like Trina, we are called to evict those thoughts. Fear doesn't belong in the spaces meant for peace. Doubt doesn't belong in a heart filled with trust. We can't sleep well, live fully, or love freely while bitterness lives where God's joy should be.

Trusting God is essential—not just in crisis, but every day. Removing the "monsters" from the heart is a process. It requires intention. But as Trina came to understand, we don't have to feel insecure about entrusting our lives to God. He has already overcome the enemy. The battle was won at the cross. Now, the real victory is claiming peace.

And best of all, Trina realized that God's promises are personal. They're for everyone—and they can be tested and trusted. Time and time again, she had to choose to believe. And time and time again, God proved faithful.

This was only the beginning of Trina's journey—but even from the start, she knew one thing: trusting God would be the key to every breakthrough.

Life Alone

In the vibrant city of San Diego, Trina had been living for five years. On the outside, her life appeared steady—she had a job, a routine, and a sense of independence. But beneath the surface, she quietly wrestled with uncertainty, doubt, and the relentless pressure to have it all figured out. The lies whispered to her daily: *You're not enough. You'll never get it right. You're on your own.*

Yet deep within her spirit, she longed for more. Not just clarity for her future, but a peace that surpassed understanding—a promise given in Philippians 4:7:

"And the peace of God, which surpasses all understanding, will guard your hearts and your minds in Christ Jesus."

Each day brought a new challenge, and Trina found herself overwhelmed by the weight of making the "right" decisions. She desperately wanted to walk in wisdom. James 1:5 became her lifeline:

"If any of you lacks wisdom, let him ask of God, who gives to all generously and without reproach, and it will be given to him."

So she asked—again and again. Through whispered prayers and tearful mornings, Trina poured her heart out to God. She leaned into her faith like tuning a radio dial, searching for His voice amidst the noise of the world. Through Scripture and worship, she began to hear Him more clearly.

As she surrendered her fears and doubts, God began to respond in ways she didn't expect. A chance encounter with a stranger who spoke the truth. A verse that jumped off the page at the exact moment she needed it. A quiet confirmation whispered into her heart. Trina was learning that Psalm 32:8 was a personal promise:

"I will instruct you and teach you in the way you should go; I will counsel you with my loving eye on you."

With each step, her faith deepened. Though her circumstances didn't always change immediately, her confidence in God did. She began to see that she didn't need to know the whole plan—she just needed to trust the One who did. As Proverbs 3:5–6 reminds us:

"Trust in the Lord with all your heart and lean not on your own understanding; in all your ways submit to Him, and He will make your paths straight."

God was guiding her, one day at a time. And in that trust, she began to see His fingerprints on everything. Her life became a testimony of divine alignment. Too many "coincidences" to be anything but the hand of God.

Jesus Christ, Come into my life. I invite You not only into my present—but into every part of who I am, even the parts I don't fully understand. I open my heart and my mind to You, Lord.

I invite You, Jesus, into my **subconscious memory**—into every hidden place where pain, fear, regret, or confusion still lives. Heal what needs healing. Forgive what needs forgiving. Redeem what feels lost. Cleanse what is broken. And **free me**, fully and completely, right now.

You are the Healer of all things. You are the Truth that sets me free. Your Word says in John 8:36, *"So if the Son sets you free, you will be free indeed."* I believe that promise.

Lord, show me the lies I've believed—about myself, about others, and about You. Replace them with Your truth. Help me release control and surrender everything to You. Lead me in Your wisdom. Guide me by Your Spirit. Fill me with Your peace.

I want to walk in the fullness of who You created me to be. You are the Way, the Truth, and the Life—and today, I choose to follow You with my whole heart.

In Your holy name I pray,

Amen.

Discerning

This book is for you—especially if you've struggled to follow the lead of a God who loves you, or if you've wrestled to believe He truly desires the best for you. Right now, His love is drawing you closer. The Holy Spirit is speaking—inviting you to lean in, to listen, and to trust.

Discerning God's voice begins with one powerful truth:

"My sheep listen to my voice; I know them, and they follow me." —*John 10:27*

So many of us are surrounded by noise—internal and external. But not every voice you hear in your mind is from God. Some are rooted in fear, insecurity, comparison, or even past trauma. Before we can fully follow God's lead, we must begin to disassociate from those false voices and tune into the one voice that brings life, peace, and truth.

Trina's journey of discernment brought her to this profound realization: honoring God was not just a moral duty—it was an act of deep, personal love. She discovered that honoring Him meant acknowledging His presence in every part of her life, not just on Sundays, not just in prayer, but in every word she spoke and every choice she made.

She was created to help people, to serve, and to love—just as you are created for a unique purpose. The question is: What are you called to do? Whatever the answer, the starting point is this: **Honor God wherever you are.** Use your gifts. Offer your life.

As Trina immersed herself in the Word, in church community, and in Spirit-led teachings, she began to understand that honoring God isn't about rituals—it's a lifestyle. A continuous, living sacrifice of obedience and love.

"Therefore, I urge you, brothers and sisters, in view of God's mercy, to offer your bodies as a living sacrifice, holy and pleasing to God—this is your true and proper worship." —*Romans 12:1*

In her everyday life, Trina sought to honor Him by choosing integrity over convenience, compassion over reaction, humility over pride. Whether in quiet conversations or bold decisions, she aimed to reflect the love of Christ. And the more she walked this path, the deeper her love for God became.

She also prayed for the **Baptism of the Holy Spirit**, longing not just for knowledge, but for divine discernment. She knew she needed more than her own reasoning—she needed a **Guide**. And the Holy Spirit became her counselor, her comforter, her compass.

"But the Advocate, the Holy Spirit, whom the Father will send in My name, will teach you all things and remind you of everything I have said to you." —John 14:26

One day, while working at a new job, Trina felt a persistent tug in her heart: *Go home.* But logic pushed back—*You have a job. Responsibilities.* Still, the nudge didn't leave her. She prayed, offering it to God.

And that very day—she lost her job.

She didn't panic. She obeyed.

She flew home to Washington, D.C., and what she found confirmed the Spirit's prompt: her father was about to undergo cancer surgery, and her mother was quietly suffering from stress-induced health issues. Trina stayed for two weeks. She ran errands, made coffee, watched movies in bed with them, and simply loved them—with her time, her laughter, her presence.

And in return, she experienced something irreplaceable: a deep and lasting **peace**—the kind that only comes from walking in the will of God.

"You will keep in perfect peace those whose minds are steadfast, because they trust in you." —Isaiah 26:3

Discernment begins with stillness. Pay attention to the voices that creep in—those that are critical, shaming, confusing, or insecure. Those voices are not from your Father in Heaven. God speaks in love, even when He corrects. His conviction never condemns—it lifts.

Trina began to discern the difference. She began to recognize when the Holy Spirit was whispering truth and when the enemy was trying to derail her with doubt. Scripture became her anchor. Worship became her reset. Obedience became her weapon.

"And you, who once were alienated and enemies in your mind by wicked works, yet now He has reconciled in the body of His flesh through death, to present you holy, and blameless, and above reproach in His sight." —Colossians 1:21–22

She had been **reconciled**. Not just to a better life—but to a better purpose.

Discerning God's voice is more than spiritual maturity—it's spiritual survival. It is how we remain tethered to truth in a world filled with deception.

God gives us the honor of hearing Him—and following Him into the life only **He** could design. We are not meant to guess our way through this life. We are meant to **walk with the Shepherd**.

Heavenly Father,

I come before You with a quieted heart, asking You to remove every voice that is not Yours. Silence the noise of doubt, fear, and confusion, and awaken my spirit to hear You clearly. I desire to know Your voice—the still, small voice that brings peace, direction, and truth.

Lord, I invite Your Holy Spirit into every part of my life. Be my Counselor, my Comforter, my Guide. Teach me to distinguish between what is true and what is a lie, between Your promptings and my own assumptions.

"Speak, Lord, for Your servant is listening."—*1 Samuel 3:10*

Forgive me for the times I followed my own understanding rather than Your leading. I surrender my need to control and my fear of not knowing what's next. I declare Your Word over my life:

"Trust in the Lord with all your heart and lean not on your own understanding; in all your ways acknowledge Him, and He will direct your path."—*Proverbs 3:5–6*

Help me honor You—not just with my words, but with my decisions, my actions, my thoughts. Let my life reflect Your glory and bring others closer to Your heart.

If there are any lies I've believed about who I am, or who You are, expose them in the light of Your love. Replace them with truth.

"You will know the truth, and the truth will set you free."—*John 8:32*

Lord, I ask for wisdom—not just knowledge, but the kind of wisdom that comes from heaven.

"But the wisdom from above is first pure, then peaceable, gentle, open to reason, full of mercy and good fruits, impartial and sincere."—*James 3:17*

Give me the courage to obey even when the path is uncertain, and the grace to follow You even when it's hard.

I belong to You. I trust You. And I will follow where You lead.

In Jesus' mighty name,

Amen.

The ULTIMATE Form of Trust: HONOR

There is a deeper kind of trust—one that moves beyond belief and into action. That trust is called honor.

To honor God is to recognize Him as Lord in all things: not just when it's easy, not just when we're in need—but when we're blessed, when we're uncertain, when we're asked to surrender. True honor is the *ultimate form of trust* because it places God first—above our emotions, our timing, our logic, even our desires.

"Those who honor me I will honor, but those who despise me will be disdained." —1 Samuel 2:30

Trina's journey taught her that trust wasn't just a feeling—it was a posture of the heart. She learned that when she honored God with her honesty, her struggles, and her obedience, He responded with open doors, unexpected provision, and deep inner peace.

Honoring God means choosing His way, even when ours feels safer. It means believing that *His thoughts are higher than our thoughts*, and His timing is perfect—even when it feels delayed. Trina had to learn this firsthand.

At one point, she was trusting God while her father battled cancer for the fifth time. She was also praying about a new job and wrestling with self-doubt. In that season, she was vulnerable with someone about her fears. She admitted what she was holding back—her "excuses." But instead of judgment, something surprising happened. The person responded with kindness and an offer to help. That simple moment—one that could have been missed—became transformative. It was an answer to prayer.

"The Lord is close to the brokenhearted and saves those who are crushed in spirit." —Psalm 34:18

In being honest, in honoring God through her humility, Trina unlocked breakthrough. Her vulnerability allowed someone else to step in as an instrument of God's grace. That's what honor does—it *invites Heaven* into the ordinary.

In that season, Trina also faced a deeper tension: she was torn between staying in San Diego and going home to her family. Her heart longed to be near them—2,700 miles away. Her spirit whispered that God had placed her where she was, but her emotions felt unstable.

So she did the only thing she could: she prayed for the power of God to help her.

Honor is surrender. Honor says, *I trust You, God, even when I don't understand You.*

Trina began to see that her feelings were not the final authority—God's promises were. She shifted from self-doubt to Spirit-led confidence. Every time she said, *"Yes, Lord,"* even when it was hard, heaven moved on her behalf.

"For those who honor me, I will honor." (1 Samuel 2:30 again—worth repeating.)

Honor also meant watching her words. She began declaring truth over her life:

"Jesus Christ is in absolute control of this situation, and Jesus Christ is producing perfect results in this matter now."

That declaration became a weapon in her spiritual arsenal.

One of the greatest realizations Trina had was this: when she honored God with her trust, He honored her with His presence. He brought clarity. He sent help. He realigned her path.

♪ Prayer of Honor and Trust

Heavenly Father,

You are worthy of my trust. Today, I choose to honor You—not just in what I say, but in how I live. I place You above my plans, my fears, my emotions, and my expectations.

Help me to live with a heart that honors You in everything. Let my trust be more than belief—let it become surrender.

"Trust in the Lord with all your heart and lean not on your own understanding." —Proverbs 3:5

I declare today that Jesus Christ is in control of my situation. You are producing perfect results in this matter, right now. Even if I can't see it yet—I believe it.

Expose anything in me that has been honoring fear instead of faith. Show me how to release every excuse, every delay, every hidden doubt. You see me completely, and You still choose to work through me. Thank You.

Give me boldness to obey. Give me discernment to follow. And give me a heart that honors You all the days of my life.

In the mighty name of Jesus,

Amen.

Entrusting

To **entrust** something is to release control—to place it with someone who is capable, faithful, and strong. And there is no one more worthy of our trust than our Heavenly Father.

"Commit your way to the Lord; trust in Him, and He will act." —*Psalm 37:5*

Trina learned this truth in one of the most unpredictable moments of her life—while white-water rafting in Colombia. She was with family, enjoying the rush of the river, when suddenly her raft hit a rock and she was thrown into the water. Disoriented and submerged, she couldn't tell which way was up. Panic set in. Her instincts screamed, *Swim!*—but she had no direction. She flailed and kicked, trapped in the unknown.

That moment became a metaphor for her spiritual life.

So many times, Trina had felt just like that—adrift, overwhelmed, unsure of which way to turn. But in that terrifying moment on the river, something shifted. The Holy Spirit led her upward, lifting her from fear to breath again.

"When you pass through the waters, I will be with you; and through the rivers, they shall not overwhelm you." —*Isaiah 43:2*

Her physical rescue mirrored a deeper truth: **God rescues us when we surrender our striving and listen for His voice.**

Our hearts can take us in the wrong direction when they're driven by fear or frustration. But when we entrust our lives to God, we invite a Father who does not manipulate, abandon, or fail. He is the One who formed us, who designed us with purpose, and who knows the path forward—even when we do not.

"Before I formed you in the womb, I knew you." —*Jeremiah 1:5*

God is not just a rescuer; He is also a Teacher. A loving Father who wants to lead us with hope and meaning. Even when the damage in our lives seems too great—even when it doesn't make sense—He is still sovereign.

Trina clung to this truth in her recovery from emotional and spiritual wounds. She remembered the promise in Ephesians 2:10:

"For we are God's masterpiece. He has created us anew in Christ Jesus, so we can do the good things He planned for us long ago."

She began to see that God often does His best work through what feels broken. He works through weakness. He carries what we can't. He commissions us to walk in healing. But first, we must reveal the very thing we'd rather hide.

As Pastor Michael Todd once said:

"You can't heal what you don't reveal."

God was guiding Trina all along—even in moments that felt like loss or chaos. He was leading her to deeper surrender. And in those moments of letting go, she began to find true freedom.

This wasn't about giving up her responsibilities—but about releasing what she couldn't control. She was learning to walk like Jesus did—in trust, in obedience, in alignment with the Father.

Even Samson, whose story was marred by disobedience, saw God's redemptive power in the end. Despite all his failures, God fulfilled His purpose through him. Why? Because God's grace is greater than our mistakes.

"My grace is sufficient for you, for My power is made perfect in weakness." —2 Corinthians 12:9

Trina began to lean into that grace. She let it shape her decisions and soften her heart. She learned that trust isn't a one-time decision—it's a rhythm. A daily turning over of fear, of timelines, of outcomes.

And every time she gave God more of her heart, she found more of His love waiting for her.

🕯 Prayer of Entrusting

Father God,

You are trustworthy and true. I release to You everything I've been holding too tightly—every fear, every timeline, every burden. I place it all into Your hands.

I surrender what I can't control. I give You the situations that feel too heavy, too broken, or too far gone. You are not overwhelmed. You are not limited. And You are not late.

"Cast all your anxiety on Him because He cares for you." —1 Peter 5:7

Holy Spirit, lead me. Help me to listen, not rush. Help me to trust, not strive. If I've been swimming against Your current, redirect my heart. Let me rise again—not in my strength, but in Yours.

Let me entrust my past to Your grace, my present to Your guidance, and my future to Your promise. I believe You are working even when I can't see it. Teach me to rest in that.

In Jesus' mighty name,

Amen.

Seek Him

There are countless distractions in this world—critical thoughts, envy, fear, insecurity—that pull us away from God's voice and drain our spiritual strength. These distractions not only cloud our peace but often manifest physically as anxiety, fatigue, or even illness. But there is a cure: **seek Him**.

"You will seek Me and find Me, when you seek Me with all your heart."
—Jeremiah 29:13

Trina began to realize that when doors opened unexpectedly or circumstances shifted, it was an invitation—not to fear, but to seek. God was drawing her closer. Every disruption became a gentle whisper: *"Come find Me in this."*

Her heart was being shaped, but first, it had to be softened. There were lies she had believed—many of them rooted in childhood or passed down through well-meaning people. One painful comment from her father had stuck with her: *"God is too busy."* It caused her to wonder: *If God is too busy, then how can He really care about me?*

But Trina brought those questions to God—raw and real. And what she discovered changed everything. God wasn't too busy. He was attentive, present, personal. He wasn't just hearing her—He was answering her.

"The eyes of the Lord are on the righteous, and His ears are attentive to their cry." —Psalm 34:15

As she sought Him more intentionally, she began to see Him working through people—ordinary moments filled with divine meaning. She realized God uses others as His hands and feet. And when He sends help, we're called to receive it.

One of the most powerful shifts in Trina's life came through a simple question:

What would I regret not doing if I looked back 20 or 40 years from now?

This question helped her tune out the voices of fear and urgency and tune into the still voice of God.

She started to picture her heart like a book—each day, a new page. And she began inviting God into every chapter. Sometimes the pages were messy, with scribbles and questions and tears. But she let Him in—knowing that even the edits would be done with grace.

She discovered that even when she had no words to describe what she felt, God understood.

🕊 A Practice of Spiritual Protection

Each morning, Trina began declaring spiritual protection—not just over herself, but over those she loved:

"I am surrounded by the pure white light of Christ. I am free from the negative thoughts of others."

"You are surrounded by the pure white light of Christ. I pronounce you free from the negative thoughts of others."

She would rise each day and entrust it to God's keeping. She prayed:

"I release this day to divine protection. God is in charge, and only good shall come from this experience. Everyone involved shall be divinely satisfied and blessed."

As fear began to fade, peace took root. God reminded her that He is not distant. He walks beside His children—even through storms.

"Even though I walk through the valley of the shadow of death, I will fear no evil, for You are with me." —Psalm 23:4

When she feared for her loved ones, she returned to this truth: **God is a protective Father.** He sees. He knows. He acts. And He never leaves.

🙏 Prayer of Seeking

Father God,

You say that if I seek You, I will find You. So today, with all my heart, I come to seek Your face. Not just Your help—but *You.* I want to know Your heart. I want to walk in Your truth.

Remove anything in me that resists Your presence. Silence the voices that shame, condemn, or confuse me. Let Your voice be louder than all of them.

You are not too busy. You are near. Your Word says:

"Draw near to God, and He will draw near to you." —James 4:8

Lord, draw near.

I surrender every burden, every question, every unanswered prayer. I give You my full attention. I invite You into the pages of my heart—the parts written, the parts still being formed.

Teach me how to live each day in pursuit of Your presence. Let me rest in the safety of Your nearness, and walk boldly in the direction of Your will.

In Jesus' holy name,

Amen.

FREEDOM

New Wine, New Life

When God began moving in Trina's heart, everything shifted. What once felt acceptable—patterns of thinking, habits of control, moments of fear—no longer had a place in her spirit. God was doing something new.

She remembered the words of Jesus in **Luke 5:37–38**

"And no one pours new wine into old wineskins. Otherwise, the new wine will burst the skins; the wine will run out and the wineskins will be ruined. No, new wine must be poured into new wineskins."

It clicked.

If God wanted to pour new life, new vision, and new purpose into her, He couldn't do it within the old framework. Trina had to be transformed—renewed from the inside out. She couldn't hold on to old thinking and expect to carry new blessings.

This was more than spiritual symbolism. This was an invitation to freedom.

Letting Go to Be Made New

Trina surrendered it all—her finances, relationships, career, even her daily decisions. She was no longer trying to manage everything by her own strength. She wanted God's wisdom to lead her, His peace to anchor her, and His love to define her future.

And it was in that surrender that she discovered freedom wasn't the absence of pressure—it was the presence of trust. Trust that God would catch her. Trust that He saw what she couldn't.

Trust that He was enough.

Every Obstacle Has a Purpose

Like many of us, Trina once believed that if she was facing opposition, she must be doing something wrong. But over time, God showed her something more powerful:

"Every problem has a promise." — Graham Cooke

The storms she faced weren't always attacks—they were often assignments. Training grounds. Opportunities to lean in closer to the Father. She began to understand that her wilderness wasn't punishment; it was **preparation**.

God had already prepared the way ahead of her.

"You hem me in behind and before, and you lay your hand upon me." — *Psalm 139:5*

"All the days ordained for me were written in your book before one of them came to be." — *Psalm 139:16*

The Test Becomes a Testimony

It didn't take long for Trina to realize that her healing, her breakthrough, her transformation—it wasn't just for her.

"Whatever you have learned or received or heard from me—or seen in me—put it into practice. And the God of peace will be with you." — *Philippians 4:9*

God was shaping her into a **living testimony**. Not a perfect person—but a **redeemed** one.

She knew that when she overcame a battle, it became a weapon in her hands to help someone else fight theirs. Her scars carried stories. Her pain carried purpose.

You Are Anointed

"As for you, the anointing you received from Him remains in you..." — *1 John 2:27*

Trina wasn't trying to be special—she was simply available. And when you're available, God can do the impossible. The more she leaned into Him, the more she saw doors open, hearts soften, and people drawn to the light inside her.

She had gone from surviving to **walking in her anointing**.

And that's the kind of freedom no one can take away.

Devotional Reflection

Freedom isn't about doing whatever you want. It's about being who God created you to be—without fear, shame, or striving.

God is constantly inviting you into more: more trust, more joy, more identity, more purpose. But in order to receive the *new wine*, the *old wineskin* must go.

That means letting go of:

- Old stories you've told yourself.

- Old lies you believed.

- Old habits that kept you stuck.

Freedom is a gift, but it starts with surrender.

Journaling Prompts

Take a few quiet moments with these questions. Let God speak to your heart.

1. What "old wineskins" might God be asking you to let go of right now?

2. Where in your life do you feel resistance—but sense He is preparing you?

3. What past struggle could become part of your testimony for someone else?

4. Have you surrendered your decisions—big or small—to God recently?

5. What does freedom in Christ mean to you today, in this season?

Guided Prayer: A Declaration of Freedom

Father God,

I thank You that I don't have to strive.

You have already prepared the way.

I release to You everything I've held too tightly—

My plans, my fears, my relationships, my past.

Pour out Your new wine in me.

Make me a new vessel.

Thank You that You have called me, chosen me, and anointed me.

What I've walked through was not wasted.

It is shaping me for a greater purpose.

I believe that every problem carries a promise.

I receive that promise now—

A promise of peace, identity, joy, and breakthrough.

I am free.

I am loved.

I am Yours.

In Jesus' mighty name,

Amen.

When Change Comes, Faith Leads

Whenever Trina moved cities or shifted careers, she no longer fell into fear or doubt. In the past, uncertainty would have left her anxious, asking, *"Why does this keep happening?"* But now, she found herself declaring:

"Thank You, Lord, that You have a great opportunity for me. I do not doubt that You truly know what is best for me. You said "You've promised to prosper me and give me hope and a future." — Jeremiah 29:11

This shift in mindset changed everything.

She had learned to **surrender her desires** to God, trusting that He truly knew what was for her. And over time, she began to live out key mindsets that built her faith:

- **What is real is often invisible** — the visible is only temporary.

- God speaks especially when we feel shame or are overlooked.

- He elevates those who humble themselves.

- We must hold fast to the truth, or the enemy will feed us lies.

Trina saw that lingering on the promises of God was vital. Otherwise, untruths would sneak in and sabotage her peace. She came to understand that one of the devil's greatest tactics was distraction—pulling her away from belief, from rest, from presence.

But the more she **rested in God**, the more clearly she heard His heart:

"I do not keep a record of wrongs. I have mercy, compassion, and healing for every wound."

She held on to the truth of Psalm 51:

"Have mercy on me, O God, according to Your unfailing love; according to Your great compassion, blot out my transgressions... cleanse me from my sin."

And she often reminded herself of Romans 8:28:

"We know that in all things God works for the good of those who love Him and are called according to His purpose."

The Shift in San Diego

When Trina moved to San Diego, she faced a housing crisis—she had just two days to find a new place to live. Logic couldn't fix the situation. So, she did what faith required: she stepped out in trust.

Even with no clear solution, she chose to believe. She reminded herself that God had provided before—and He would again. She called her mom and spoke words of faith out loud, even when she only had a faint inner conviction. Her declaration became her direction.

At the time, she had been staying in a beautiful $1.5 million condo overlooking the bay in Crown Point—a space generously offered by a friend. It had been a season of rest, of recalibration. But when her friend's family needed the space back, Trina had to leave, fast.

She didn't panic. She packed a few essentials, made some calls, and stayed focused on her promise: **"A miracle is going to happen."**

She called eight friends, simply telling them what she believed: **"God will provide."**

And He did. One friend had a room available for a full month—no strings attached. When Trina arrived, she noticed something powerful: the space was filled with **elephant figurines**—eleven of them, to be exact. For her, elephants had always been a personal symbol of divine guidance and strength. It was confirmation. She was right where she was meant to be.

From Crisis to Redemption

During this season, she also navigated an unexpected roommate conflict. Her previous roommate had asked her to leave, overwhelmed by inner guilt and unresolved shame. He had made the space unsafe.

Trina had felt prompted to speak truth gently before she left:

"God loves you no matter what."

At the time, it seemed like her words fell flat. But weeks later, she learned he had checked himself into rehab—and there, he received Jesus into his heart.

She hadn't tried to fix him. She had simply spoken life.

Faith for the Impossible

"This poor man called, and the Lord heard him; He saved him out of all his troubles." — *Psalm 34:4*

Trina kept practicing a bold mindset: **"LORD, help me never be afraid of the impossible."**

She brought God into every situation. And over time, she began to recognize Him in people, in conversations, in divine timing.

She reflected on how Jesus spoke to the woman at the well in **John 4**— gently, directly, lovingly. He offered her something deeper than momentary relief:

"Whoever drinks of the water that I give will never thirst… It will become a fountain springing up into everlasting life."

That's what she wanted more than anything: **living water.**

Not surface-level peace. Not temporary fixes. **Real transformation.**

Letting God Reframe Our Lives

As Trina reflected on her journey, she began to see how God had been reframing her perspectives—especially in moments of loss, confusion, or change.

She journaled:

- **"Your mistake is a redirection."**
- **"Make the devil scared and leave!"** — a quote from her pastor, Jon Heindriks.

She realized she had been living to prove herself—to be accepted, seen, validated. But now, she wanted something deeper. She wanted to help others, to connect, to understand. She wanted to see life from others' eyes, not just her own.

At a local coffee shop, she reflected:

"I want to enjoy conversation. I want to be open. Everyone's so different— what a gift to learn from one another."

Surrender and Trust

Trina knew that the journey with God often begins with one step: **surrender.**

Sometimes it's hard to know where to start. But even five minutes with God in the morning—before the day gets busy—can shift everything.

She remembered Hebrews 13:5:

"Don't be obsessed with getting more material things. Be relaxed with what you have." (MSG)

If you're holding on to **unanswered prayers**, start with forgiveness. Forgiveness releases you to let go—and let God.

Revelation That Changes You

"If then you have been raised with Christ, seek the things above… For you died, and your life is hidden with Christ in God." — Colossians 3:1–3

Trina learned to **set her mind on things above.** To let go of shallow pursuits and step into deeper truth. She believed that the **revelation of Christ** would rise in us—if we made space for it.

She revisited the story of Job—how Job asked for forgiveness and was restored.

"The Lord restored his prosperity and gave him twice as much as before." — Job 42

It reminded her: what she had lost wasn't random. God had removed what no longer served her so He could give her something greater.

A Journey of Trust

Trina's life became a story of **faith in motion.** She wanted others to know: **this kind of trust is available to everyone.** But it requires movement. It requires saying "yes" when you'd rather stay safe.

She prayed:

"God, don't let me become too comfortable to obey Your call. Let me trust You more than I trust my plans. Let me believe You for the impossible."

Devotional Reflection

Ask yourself:

- Where do I need to trust God more?

- Am I holding on to an "old wineskin" in my mindset, fears, or habits?

- What miracle am I believing for today?

Journaling Prompts

1. When have I seen God provide when I didn't know how things would work out?

2. What symbols or signs (like Trina's elephants) has God used to confirm His presence?

3. Am I open to seeing God in others—even those who seem difficult?

4. What would surrender look like for me this week?

Guided Prayer

Father God, Thank You for every shift You allow in my life—whether it feels like a loss or a rescue. Help me to walk in trust, even when the path is unclear. Teach me to surrender—not out of defeat, but out of faith. You are my living water. You are my way through impossible circumstances. You restore what is broken. And You are writing a better story than I could ever write for myself.

Open my eyes to the signs, the people, and the quiet reminders that You are near. Let me see You in every detail. I choose to believe again. In Jesus' name,

Amen.

Overcoming in Power

When Faith Leads the Way

Every time Trina faced change—whether moving to a new city or stepping into a different job—she anchored herself in truth. In the past, uncertainty would have overwhelmed her. But now, she had a different mindset.

Instead of asking, *"Why does this keep happening?"* She began to declare,

"Thank You, Lord, that You have a great opportunity for me. I do not doubt that You truly know what is best for me. You promised to prosper me and give me hope and a future." — Jeremiah 29:11

This shift in her thinking became her strength. She had learned to surrender her desires to God, trusting that His plan was better—even when the path was unclear.

Mindsets That Shape the Journey

There were several truths that Trina held close—lessons that had become spiritual anchors for her soul:

- Everything real is in the invisible—what is seen is temporary.

- God speaks most powerfully when we feel shame or undervalued.

- He doesn't elevate based on performance—but on surrender.

- What you choose to believe will either strengthen you or deceive you.

The enemy's greatest weapon, she had learned, was distraction. If the enemy could get her to forget who God was—or who she was in Him—he could derail her peace.

But the more Trina lingered in God's presence, the more she saw clearly: God doesn't keep a record of wrongs. He offers mercy, healing, and renewal.

"Have mercy on me, O God, according to your unfailing love… blot out my transgressions." — Psalm 51

She learned to return often to this verse—and also to the promise in Romans 8:28:

"And we know that in all things God works for the good of those who love Him and are called according to His purpose."

A Shift in San Diego

One of the most defining moments of trust came when Trina found herself unexpectedly without a place to stay in San Diego. She had only two days to figure out her living situation, and no concrete plan in sight.

Instead of panicking, she chose to believe.

She stepped out of her logical thinking and into faith. She had seen God provide before, and she reminded herself of that truth. She even told her mom, with a quiet but determined conviction, *"This is going to work out."*

She had been staying in a stunning $1.5 million condo in Crown Point, graciously offered by a friend. When that space was needed back for family, Trina knew it was time to move on—with gratitude, not fear.

She packed a few essentials, called a handful of people, and spoke boldly:

"A miracle is going to happen."

And it did.

One friend happened to have a room available and offered it to her for a full month. When Trina walked in, she immediately sensed God's confirmation. There were **elephant figurines** scattered around the room—eleven of them. For Trina, elephants had long symbolized strength, memory, and divine guidance. It was a personal sign that she was exactly where she was meant to be.

Ministry in the Middle of Conflict

Around the same time, Trina experienced an emotional and spiritual test with a roommate. Tension had escalated, and the living environment had become unsafe. The roommate, consumed by guilt and shame over his past, asked her to leave.

Instead of reacting with anger, Trina responded with truth:

"God loves you no matter what."

She left in peace. Weeks later, she learned that he had checked into a rehabilitation center—and during his stay, he gave his life to Jesus.

She hadn't tried to change him. But her presence, her words, and her example had planted a seed.

Faith for the Impossible

Trina adopted a bold new declaration: **"LORD, help me never be afraid of the impossible."**

She practiced bringing God into every moment, every unknown, every decision. And in doing so, she began to see Jesus in people and circumstances all around her.

"This poor man called, and the Lord heard him; He saved him out of all his troubles." — Psalm 34:6

She remembered how Jesus spoke to the woman at the well in John 4. He didn't shame her. He offered her something deeper.

"Whoever drinks of the water that I give will never thirst again... It will become a fountain springing up into everlasting life."

That's what Trina longed for. Not surface-level peace. Not temporary solutions. **Living water. Lasting change. True power.**

When God Reframes Your Story

As she reflected on her journey, Trina began to see how God had been reframing her life—not just adjusting her circumstances, but transforming her understanding.

She heard God whisper:

"Your mistake is a redirection."

She recalled her pastor, Jon Heindriks, once saying:

"Make the devil scared and leave!"

She had spent so much of her early life trying to prove her worth—to be seen, accepted, and applauded. But now, she wanted more. She wanted to serve others, to listen well, to live a life of **purpose over performance**.

Sitting in a coffee shop, she thought: *"I want to enjoy deep conversation. I want to understand people, not fix them. I want to hear new perspectives and grow."*

Her heart was open. And that was a win.

Power in Surrender

Trina had come to believe that true power is found in **surrender**. Even five quiet minutes with God in the morning could reset her entire day. She clung to this promise:

"Don't be obsessed with getting more material things. Be relaxed with what you have." — Hebrews 13:5 (MSG)

When she found herself wrestling with **unanswered prayers**, she learned to begin with **forgiveness**—forgiving others, forgiving herself, and releasing the outcome to God.

"He looks at us with mercy." — Psalm 123

The Revelation That Changes Everything

"If you have been raised with Christ, seek the things above… For your life is hidden with Christ in God." — Colossians 3:1–3

Trina began to truly **set her mind on things above**. She no longer wanted to live at surface level. She wanted to rise into the reality of who Christ had made her to be.

She revisited the story of **Job**, who, after suffering unimaginable loss, asked for forgiveness and was fully restored.

"The Lord blessed the latter part of Job's life more than the former." — Job 42

It reminded her that God restores what we thought was permanently lost. Every surrendered loss became a seed for greater blessing.

Living a Life of Power and Purpose

Now, Trina sees her life as a testimony of choices—small, faithful decisions to **trust God**, over and over again. This kind of trust isn't loud or flashy. It's persistent. It's quiet. And it's powerful.

She knows now:

- God takes the broken pieces and builds something better.
- God uses the impossible to birth the incredible.
- God always, always keeps His promises.

Her prayer became:

"God, don't let me be too comfortable to follow Your voice. Don't let me settle when You're calling me higher. Give me the courage to believe again."

Reflection

"Overcoming in Power" isn't about never struggling. It's about learning to trust in the struggle. It's about choosing to see God's hand even in the dark.

Devotional Prompts

1. Where have I been afraid of the unknown? Can I invite God into it?

2. What signs or symbols has God used to speak to me personally?

3. In what areas do I need to trade striving for surrender?

4. Who in my life has changed simply because I chose to speak truth in love?

Guided Prayer

Heavenly Father,

I thank You that You never waste a trial.

I trust You in the transitions, the losses, the redirections.

You are with me. You are for me.

Help me to live boldly and believe fiercely.

Help me to listen well, speak truth, and love deeply.

I choose today to overcome in Your power—not my own.

I will not fear the impossible.

Because I know that with You, **all things are possible.**

In Jesus' name,

Amen.

Guiding Ourselves

There are moments in life when everything feels like it's falling apart—and those are often the moments God uses to guide us. They don't make sense at first. Chaos swirls. Clarity fades. The noise of disappointment, uncertainty, and fear grows louder.

But even in the thick of it, God whispers: **"I'm here."**

Alex's Turning Point

Alex was thirty, successful, and outwardly thriving. He had built a respected company on the East Coast. But under the surface, he was quietly unraveling. The pressure to maintain appearances and performance left him hollow. Depression crept in unnoticed—until it consumed his thoughts.

One day, he got in his car and drove west. Mile after mile, the city faded. The silence grew louder. And the question that echoed in his soul: **What's the point of it all?**

Externally accomplished. Internally empty.

Somewhere along that desert highway, something shifted. In the middle of his mental storm, Alex made a decision: **"I won't let these thoughts define me."**

He turned the car around. Not to escape, but to return—to faith, to stillness, to truth.

Back East, he reconnected with spiritual roots. He pressed into the Word. He allowed God to meet him in the silence. And when he returned West, it wasn't to chase success—it was to walk in peace. He hadn't just reversed his route. **He had reclaimed his identity.**

Not everyone understood. But that didn't matter. Because when God calls you back to Himself, your path may look different—but it will lead to freedom.

Trina and the Garden of Forgiveness

In the quiet coastal town of Willow Creek, Trina was known for her bold independence. Her beachside life was built on self-reliance and routine. But God had more in store.

One afternoon, she met Mrs. Eileen Thompson—a woman with a gentle smile, wise eyes, and the most fragrant white plumeria flowers. Their friendship began with casual conversation and blossomed into something sacred.

Eileen noticed Trina's guardedness—especially when things didn't go her way. Trina was strong, but beneath the strength was resentment. Disappointments had piled up, and she had learned to protect herself by staying in control.

But Eileen, with grace and tenderness, helped her see another way **Forgiveness wasn't weakness—it was release.**

At first, Trina resisted. Vulnerability felt risky. But as their conversations deepened, so did her healing. Layer by layer, she began to confront the wounds she had buried. And with each layer surrendered, her heart softened.

Eileen reminded her,

"When triggers resurface, it's not punishment—it's an invitation. God is calling you to heal, not hide."

Trina realized that much of her pain came from seeking external validation in the absence of inner love. So she began asking new questions:

- What if I let the thoughts come instead of shoving them down?
- What if I asked God to show me the moment that broke me?
- What if healing started with honest conversations—with Him, and with myself?

And it did.

Learning to Listen Again

Trina began to pull inward. She started listening to the quiet center of her heart. There, she found clarity. Like spinning the wheel in prayer, God would highlight the next right step. No big signs, just sacred nudges.

Just as Moses' staff held notches—memories of God's faithfulness—Trina began to mark her journey with spiritual moments. Every surrendered resentment became a stone of remembrance.

"I trust in God's unfailing love forever and ever." — Psalm 52:8

"I am the vine; you are the branches. If you remain in me and I in you, you will bear much fruit..." — *John 15:5*

She learned that **surrender isn't automatic**—it's intentional. And if we ignore what's buried deep, it resurfaces when we least expect it.

Surrender isn't denial. It's **making space** for God to speak.

The Power of Honest Questions

Letting go doesn't mean giving up. It means giving over.

Giving your burdens to God. Giving your disappointments permission to be healed.

Questions like:

- Did they want more from me than I could give?

- What do I need to release to move forward?

These aren't just reflections. They're doorways to **healing**.

The goal isn't perfection. It's belief. Believing that change is possible. That you're not too late. That nothing is wasted.

A New Way Forward

Trina developed a mindset that became her compass:

- Trust in prayer

- Trust the process

- Be patient with yourself

- Endure—because character is built in the waiting

She reflected:

"I used to think I had to work hard and make it happen. Then I began saying, 'God, I need You. Please show Yourself here.' Now I say, 'God, here's the desire of my heart—spoken and unspoken. Surprise me with what You've prepared.'"

She had learned what whitewater rafting teaches: **don't resist the current—lean into it.**

The current of God's love carries us. And when we stop striving and start trusting, we find our footing.

Anchored in Scripture, Surrounded by Grace

Scripture became Trina's anchor. She wrote verses on 3x5 cards. She placed them where her eyes would fall during the day—reminders of hope, of truth, of strength.

She gave her pain to God. She laid down the chains of self-protection and whispered, **"This isn't mine anymore."**

And God met her there—in the quiet, in the wrestling, in the trust.

The Invitation

Let God guide you. Let Him meet you in the moment.

He's not asking for perfection—**just permission**.

And when you give Him your "yes," **He gives you His peace.**

Reflection and Application

Guiding ourselves means learning to listen—first to God, then to ourselves. It means recognizing that triggers are teachers, that wounds can become altars, and that surrender is not the end—it's the doorway to **beginning again**.

Questions to Reflect On:

1. What situation in your life feels out of control? Have you invited God into it?

2. Is there someone or something you need to forgive to make room for healing?

3. What does it look like for you to surrender, practically?

4. Where might God be nudging you to pause and listen—before you act?

Guided Prayer

God,

I don't always know what to do.

But I know You do.

I give You access to every part of my heart—even the hidden ones.

Guide me. Heal me. Teach me how to trust again.

I surrender the weight of trying to figure it all out on my own.

I want to hear Your voice above the noise.

Help me let go of resentment, fear, control, and shame.

I trust that You are guiding me—even when I don't see it yet.

Surprise me with what You've prepared.

In Jesus' name,

Amen.

Confirmation

It's always a wonder to witness what God has prepared for us—especially when it exceeds anything we imagined we could accomplish.

But first, let's get one thing clear:

Rushing what takes time rarely ends well.

There is **purpose in the waiting**.

And for Trina, learning her identity in Christ had to come before anything else.

The Gift of Slow Growth

In a world that pushes us to move fast, succeed early, and keep climbing, God offers a different rhythm—one of **roots before fruit**.

Trina had to unlearn the cultural expectation of instant success and lean into a slower, sacred process. The waiting wasn't punishment. It was preparation.

God was teaching her something essential:

Before you build anything meaningful, you must first become grounded in who you are.

The waiting season forged her character.

And even when she couldn't see what was coming, God was working beneath the surface.

Work with What's in Your Hands

When we are faithful with what's in front of us—without striving or comparison—we create space for destiny to unfold.

Trina began to understand that, like love, **purpose doesn't come rushed**. It comes in **the right season**. Sometimes you have to meet the wrong people, walk through detours, or outgrow former versions of yourself before you can recognize what's truly right.

It's all part of the design.

The danger isn't in the waiting—it's in growing **weary** during the wait. Distractions will come. Doubts will whisper. But don't abandon your assignment. Stay focused.

There's a divine timeline at play. **And it's worth the wait.**

"God is not delayed. He's intentional."

Provision and People in the Waiting

Trina started noticing a pattern: Many people met their person when they weren't looking—when they were focused on growth, healing, or purpose. Few felt "ready," but God moved anyway.

She also noticed how many women around her were carrying heavy financial burdens—and how love, community, and **God's provision** often showed up together in surprising ways.

For the first time in her own life, Trina allowed herself to receive help. God sent someone to support her during a moment of real need. At first, she promised she would repay him—quickly and fully. But she soon realized: **this wasn't just about repayment.**

This was about learning to **trust God** with her heart. With her story. With her future.

The Key Was Never Control

The key wasn't obsessing over what hadn't happened.

It wasn't hustling for the next opportunity.

The key was **trust**.

Trust that God hadn't forgotten.

Trust that what was meant for her couldn't pass her by.

Trust that peace, not pressure, would guide her toward promise.

And just like that, something inside her shifted:

She didn't have to chase confirmation. It would come.

Wrapped in clarity, wrapped in peace—**wrapped in God's perfect timing.**

God's Calling Doesn't Expire

"For the gifts and the calling of God are irrevocable." — *Romans 11:29*

Trina began to rest in this truth:

What God has spoken over your life doesn't expire.

Your calling isn't canceled by your confusion.

Your gifts aren't void because of your past.

Your purpose is not revoked because of a detour.

You may have wandered.

You may have even tried to walk away.

But heaven hasn't changed its mind.

Step Into It Again

The invitation still stands.

God is still waiting for your **yes**.

Not because you feel ready—but because He's already spoken it.

Return to it.

Steward it.

Step into it again.

The path forward isn't about perfection. It's about faithfulness.

And confirmation will come—not from striving, but from surrender.

Reflection

Where are you rushing what God wants to grow slowly?

What promises has He spoken over your life that you've quietly set aside?

Questions to Consider

1. In what areas of your life do you feel tempted to rush the process?

2. Have you confused delay with denial?

3. What gift or calling have you walked away from that God might be inviting you to revisit?

4. What would it look like to live today as though God's "yes" still stands?

Guided Prayer

Father God,

Thank You for Your perfect timing.

I confess the places where I've grown impatient or discouraged.

I lay down the urge to control, to hurry, or to question what You've already promised.

I receive again the truth:

Your calling on my life hasn't changed.

Your gifts in me are still alive.

Help me stay faithful in the waiting.

Help me trust You when I cannot see.

And when Your confirmation comes, let me recognize it—wrapped in peace, covered in grace, and filled with purpose.

I believe You're working.

And I say yes again.

In Jesus' name,

Amen.

Stepping Into Your Purpose

Trina sat on her bed, sipping tea with the music turned up loud—it was her way of drowning out everything else. Music had always been a love language to her, a sacred rhythm that met her soul.

That day, her tea bag tag read:

"May your head and your heart speak with one voice."

She smiled and thought, *Wow, I love that.* She longed for that kind of unity within herself—and for the world.

Lately, though, she'd been wondering:

Why do I feel stuck? Why do I feel lost, unsure of what to do next?

Wrestling Through the Unknown

It had been a confusing season—**inexplicable at best**. Physical distress crept in more than she wanted. Sleep was interrupted. Overthinking came in waves.

And yet... she knew in her spirit that God always comes through.

But if she focused on what might go wrong, the stress would take over. Even small conversations started to feel overwhelming. Still, she knew she had to live with integrity—especially with her own heart.

Her faith was still intact, but fragile.

"I'm just borrowing a bit of other people's beliefs right now," she'd say. Sometimes, that little mustard seed was *barely there*. But it was **enough**.

Anchored by Community and Prayer

She did what she could: she showed up.

To church. To serve. To pray.

And just by being around people of faith, she found strength to do the right thing.

One Sunday, after praying for connection, she received a phone call. Her volunteer leader from the 11 AM service reached out—grieving the loss of her job and unsure how she'd make ends meet.

It was as if God had *immediately* answered Trina's prayer to be seen and supported—by letting her become the support someone else needed.

At the same time, Trina was holding onto her own burdens.

She had a car she believed was from the Lord—confirmed after she asked for a clear sign at church. But financial stress loomed.

Some days, the only peace came from remembering:

"It's okay to not know the future."

Sometimes, the only prayer she could whisper was,

"God, reveal to me what I need to know right now."

Altar Encounters & Altered Lives

She attended an altar call one Sunday where her pastor, Ps. Jurgen, said something that pierced her spirit:

"Your life will be altered when you bring it to the altar."

She responded, physically getting out of her chair and bringing her worries before God. He spoke through her pastor again:

"Just as Jesus rebuked the wind and the waves, and the storm became still— **so will your storm be calmed."**

She left that moment feeling *seen*. Covered. Supported by a church that *read her life* without her saying a word.

And most importantly—**she felt no shame**. Only peace.

A Season of Receiving Love

When she got home that day, she prayed:

"God, is my career really my purpose?"

And she sensed Him whisper back:

"For this season, your purpose is simply to feel My love."

That realization unraveled her.

She spent the next two years in a deep place of receiving God's overwhelming love. Not earning. Not performing. Just **receiving**.

Glorifying God Is the Point

She came to understand something profound:

If what you're doing doesn't point others to the Father—it may not be your true calling.

God created us to bring Him joy. To glorify Him. To live free from anxiety, fear, and shame—and to live in the **fullness of His glory**.

He will never ask you to glorify anything above Himself. Not your spouse. Not your career. Not even your calling.

"You shall have no other gods before Me." —*Exodus 20:3*

Romans 1:5 says:

"Through Christ, God has given us the privilege and authority… so that they will believe and obey Him, bringing glory to His name."

And like Abraham with Isaac in Genesis 22, Trina realized she had to be **willing to lay it all down**—even the good things.

You Were Formed with Purpose

"You saw me before I was born. Every day of my life was recorded in your book." —*Psalm 139:16*

God had already written out every chapter of her life—even the confusing ones.

He had already formed her identity, bit by bit, sculpted from nothing into someone He called **"Mine."**

Isaiah 43 echoes His heart:

"Do not fear, for I have redeemed you; I have summoned you by name; you are mine."

Aligning Purpose With Provision

Trina began praying boldly:

"I command provision and guidance in Jesus' name. Let my purpose align with my livelihood."

2 Corinthians 8:13–15 reminded her:

"Your plenty will supply what they need… their plenty will supply what you need."

Purpose isn't just about calling—it's about **trusting**. It's about believing in the "on-demand" guidance of the Holy Spirit.

She knew:

The more time you spend with God, the more direction flows like a river. Like breath.

The Epidemic of Purposelessness

Trina often pondered how few people live with a clear sense of purpose. Statistics say less than 5% can articulate it—and only 2% live aligned with it.

But we don't need a title to live on purpose. We just need clarity, surrender, and daily obedience.

Even when you don't have the full picture, you can still pray:

"Father God, remove confusion. Help me shift my thinking toward Your wisdom, Your truth. Through the power of the Holy Spirit, amen."

Worship Is for God, Not Us

Rick Warren writes in *The Purpose Driven Life*:

"Worship is not for our benefit. It's for God's."

God is not moved by ritual.

He's moved by **passion, sincerity, and surrender**.

"These people honor me with their lips, but their hearts are far from me."
—Isaiah 29:13

From Religion to Relationship

When we detox from religious fear and embrace love, something shifts.

Colossians 1:5 tells us that the true Gospel is union with God—**not separation**.

Trina began to see money, purpose, and identity all differently when she embraced this truth:

"His grace is sufficient for you."

You are meant to be free. Fully you. Fully His.

Healing, Confidence & Divine Identity

At one point, Trina wrestled with deep shame—from abuse, insecurity, and self-doubt. She felt uncomfortable in her own skin.

But over time, God used even strange dreams and inner torment to bring healing.

She remembered Carl Jung's words:

"Your vision will become clear only when you look into your heart."

Knowing your own brokenness is how you learn to love others well.

Through community, reflection, and courageous action—**Trina rebuilt her confidence.** She prayed for divine appointments, and God led her to people with the wisdom she needed.

Faith Is a Lifestyle of Obedience

When you take action—even while afraid—something changes.

Trina learned to ask questions, seek guidance, and trust that **faithful steps lead to faithful fruit.**

"I was made in the image of God. I can hear Him. I am being transformed."

"In this world you will have trouble. But take heart! I have overcome the world."—John 16:33

Hearing God Is Your Birthright

You were created for constant connection with your Creator.

That's your **birthright**.

Trina asked for three years, "God, should I go out or stay in tonight?"

And in that process, she learned that intimacy with God is the goal.

"Be still and know that I am God."—Psalm 46:10

"Come to Me and rest."—Matthew 11:28

Questions to Ponder:

- How can I be led if I'm not tuned in to hear?

- Where have I replaced purpose with performance?

- Do I believe I can hear God today?

"Now this is eternal life: that they know You, the only true God, and Jesus Christ, whom You have sent." —John 17:3

"To know this love that surpasses knowledge... and be filled with all the fullness of God." —Ephesians 3:19

You are in union with God.

You were made for purpose, peace, and power.

Let Him lead.

Let Him speak.

And let your life **glorify Him**—step by step.

In Jesus, We Have No Fear

Much like a storybook prince who goes to great lengths to defend his kingdom, we have Jesus—our victorious King—not just over one kingdom, but over all. He doesn't merely push back the darkness—He has *already conquered it*. The battle is won. And even more, He has given us the Holy Spirit to empower us as we live out that victory.

"For we do not wrestle against flesh and blood, but against principalities, against powers, against the rulers of the darkness of this age..." — *Ephesians 6:12*

If you want to witness the glory of God in action, read the Scriptures and watch how powerfully He moved—through Jesus and through His people. Miracles, deliverance, healing—it all points to a God who is alive and active. But to live fully in that power and love, we need something often forgotten: a healthy fear of the Lord.

Without it, our priorities scatter. With it, our hearts align with His.

"The Lord delights in those who fear Him, who put their hope in His unfailing love."— *Psalm 147:11*

"Do not fear those who kill the body but cannot kill the soul. Rather, fear Him who can destroy both soul and body in hell." — *Matthew 10:28*

From the very beginning, God rescued His people for the sake of His name—so His name would not be dishonored among the nations (Ezekiel 20:9). Even in Psalm 23:3, it says, "He guides me in paths of righteousness for His name's sake." Everything God does is filled with purpose—and that purpose is to reveal His character, His power, and His deep love.

Remember when Jesus healed the woman with the issue of blood? Or when He opened the eyes of the blind and cast out demons? He did these things so we would understand not only who He is—but also who *we are* in Him. Because of His Spirit in us, we are empowered to walk in the same healing and freedom.

"But very truly I tell you, it is for your good that I am going away. Unless I go, the Advocate will not come to you; but if I go, I will send Him to you." — *John 16:7*

Jesus left so the Holy Spirit could come—and the Spirit now lives in you. The Father's love is not distant. It is poured out. Tangible. Present. Near.

"Let us hold tightly without wavering to the hope we affirm, for God can be trusted to keep His promise." — Hebrews 10:23

So I declare:

"My Father has entrusted everything to me. No one truly knows the Son except the Father, and no one truly knows the Father except the Son—and those to whom the Son chooses to reveal Him." — Matthew 11:27

Jesus is willing to reveal the Father. He wants to! And so I echo that willingness: "Lord, I, too, want to reveal You to others. Use my life. Let my words be covered by the Holy Spirit, that I may declare boldly all that You've done for me."

Jesus fights for us—not just as a Prince—but as the risen King who never loses a battle. When we practice coming before the throne of grace—again and again—we will *live* in the experience of our union with Him. The more we lean in, the more we'll discover: There is no fear in love. There is no fear in Jesus.

Uncovering the Darkness

One of the greatest spiritual lessons Trina has learned is the power of *declaring and claiming* the promises of God. Something shifted the moment she began to pray *before* the sun rose. The atmosphere of her day changed. Her mind shifted. Her spirit aligned. There was something about meeting God first thing in the morning that gave her a supernatural advantage.

(See *"Command the Day"* by Dr. D.K. Olukoya for more on this principle.)

As she embraced this habit, she began to notice how deeply her understanding of her identity in Christ transformed her outlook. She wasn't just praying—she was *standing in her rightful authority.* She knew who she was. And when you live from that place—abiding in the Spirit—there's no limit to what God can do through you, as long as it aligns with His will.

"I am the vine, you are the branches. If you remain in Me and I in you, you will bear much fruit; apart from Me you can do nothing." — *John 15:5*

Even in seemingly small matters—like needing a place to live—she learned to invite God in. One time, through real financial hardship, she prayed for a miracle. That miracle came in the form of a little studio apartment just a block from the beach and the bay. The very place she had written about in her journal months before. God had hinted at it during her quiet time—and then, *He fulfilled it.*

Moments like that became her anchor. When doubt or fear crept in, she would remember the *Mission Beach studio* and think, "If He did that, He'll do it again." That's the beautiful rhythm of walking with God—you get to *know His character.* And the more she surrendered every area of her life to Him, the more she saw His fingerprints everywhere.

There was even a moment when she prayed specifically for a ladder to reach her "upper room" in her bedroom—a little nook she had set aside as her daily meeting place with God. Later that day, she randomly found the perfect ladder leaning beside a storage unit on the side of the road. A small thing? Maybe to someone else. But to her, it was a movie moment. A God moment. Her faith grew stronger with every answered prayer.

"Commit your work to the Lord, and your plans will succeed."— *Proverbs 16:3*

To her, prayer began to feel like writing a note, tying it to a helium balloon, and watching it rise into the sky. Or slipping that note into a glass bottle and releasing it into the ocean. A symbol of surrender. A declaration of trust. She believed God delights in those childlike gestures. He moves powerfully in the 1% odds, the unimaginable, the inconceivable. That's where His glory shines.

Prayer of Release

Heavenly Father, I lift my cares, my desires, and my dreams to You. I believe You planted them in my heart for a reason, and I trust You to lead me into all You have for me. I acknowledge I can do nothing apart from You. You know my heart more intimately than I do. I commit it all to You—my time, my calling, my future. Cover me with Your protection. Let God arise in every difficult situation I face. I invite Your Spirit to lead and guide me. In Jesus' name, amen.

When we intentionally seek God's covering—when we pray to be protected from temptation and spiritual distraction—*we gain the upper hand.* This is what awakened Trina to write this book. What started as a title—spoken by two different women in her weekly prayer group—became a divine assignment. As soon as she sat down to write, it became clear: this message was not just about life—it was about purpose.

God wants you to know your purpose. And more than that—He wants you to walk in it.

So what if today you made this your declaration:

"Finding and fulfilling my God-given purpose is my number one priority."

Because when you seek it—you *will* find it. When you ask—He answers. And when you commit it to Him—He will do more than you can imagine.

Converse With God

Journaling is not just a suggestion—it's a spiritual necessity.

Writing down your conversations with God creates a sacred space where your thoughts meet His voice. The Source of Life is speaking, and when you listen through writing, something powerful begins to happen.

Journaling is a form of meditation. A way of hearing God. And honestly? It can often feel more natural than trying to speak aloud. When you begin to write to Him, you might find it easier—like you're talking to a close friend. And the more consistently you journal with God, the more clearly you'll hear from Him. Healing will begin to unfold in places you didn't even know were hurting.

You'll become one of *"those who commune with God in words of wisdom."* And the beauty? That intimacy doesn't just transform you—it overflows into others.

It releases faith.

Because that's God's desire for you.

"Draw near to God, and He will draw near to you." — *James 4:8*

"I love those who love Me, and those who seek Me diligently find Me."— *Proverbs 8:17*

"If any of you lacks wisdom, let him ask God, who gives generously to all without reproach, and it will be given him." — *James 1:5*

And of course—one of Trina's personal favorites:

"Call to Me, and I will answer you and tell you great and unsearchable things you do not know." — *Jeremiah 33:3*

Trina had always been a curious soul—especially about what God might be up to behind the scenes. Maybe it was the analytical side of her. But more than anything, she just really believed... *God could be asked.*

At a young age, she found comfort in writing. It helped her process moments that felt meaningful. She would jot down inspiring quotes, observations, or notes about people who seemed uniquely placed in her life. When she had her first boyfriend—the one who took her ice skating—she wrote about how he treated her, how he made her feel safe. Same with Michael, her college love. Each journal entry captured more than a moment—it captured her journey.

But when her faith deepened—when she became a born-again believer—her journaling turned into something holy.

There was a time she found herself alone in San Diego, working to pay rent on her own. And even then, she thought:

"God, I think You hear me… because somehow You keep giving me what I need."

San Diego felt like the exact place she was meant to be.

But then, things changed. She found drugs on the kitchen floor—right in the place she called home. The atmosphere shifted, and she knew she couldn't stay. The house didn't feel safe, and she couldn't compromise on peace. When she brought it up to the young man's mother, she begged Trina not to leave. But Trina knew—this wasn't her fight. Her safety and her spiritual peace had to come first.

That night, she woke up with a relentless itch in her arm—one that no cream or Benadryl could soothe. Restless and wide awake, she spotted a pen. Something stirred in her spirit.

Write.

So she did.

She poured her heart onto the page, asking God for clarity, peace, and a new living space. She wrote about a place where she could feel safe, somewhere she could stay in San Diego without fear or compromise. And as the ink hit the page, she felt it: *God was with her.*

That journal became her altar.

That moment became a conversation.

No place would be perfect—but each place would hold lessons.

Every room would become a classroom.

And every journal entry? A divine dialogue.

She was learning to walk with God through paper and pen.

And through those conversations—she began to hear Him speak.

Wisdom is Better than Rubies!

Seriously—do you believe that? It's easy to forget, especially when life feels complicated or overwhelming. But Trina discovered a powerful truth: the beginning of faith in any hard situation starts with wisdom. And not just any kind of wisdom—the kind that is precious beyond measure, the kind that leads to clarity, peace, and transformation. The kind that only comes from God.

Trina learned early on to be cautious about the kind of wisdom she received. While people meant well, not all advice was Spirit-led. Some counsel was filtered through pain, disappointment, or even hidden motives. And that wisdom? It carried weight—sometimes hurtful, sometimes misleading. But true wisdom? It flows from the heart of Jesus, the doorkeeper of our soul. His wisdom leads to freedom, forgiveness, and healing—never bondage or bitterness.

Ephesians 6:18 reminds us, "Pray in the Spirit at all times and on every occasion. Stay alert and be persistent in your prayers for all believers everywhere." This is wisdom in action. It's a posture of prayer, alertness, and perseverance. Wisdom also means knowing who you are in Christ. Jeremiah 1:5 declares, "I knew you before I formed you in your mother's womb. Before you were born, I set you apart and appointed you as my prophet to the nations."

Trina cherished verses like these. She clung to the Word as her compass. 1 Corinthians 13 reminded her that wisdom is love in action—it keeps no record of wrongs. Proverbs 3:5-6 taught her to trust God, even when she couldn't see the next step. And the call to honor her parents in Exodus 20 and Ephesians 6 helped her recognize how foundational respect and obedience are to a life of blessing.

She loved the Bible more than rubies—literally. She once lost a cherished ruby, and it bothered her deeply. But the thought of losing the Word of God? That was unthinkable. The Scriptures became her lifeline, her conversation starter with God.

Quick Reflection: How do you stay on track in life?

The Bible is filled with stories that speak directly into our everyday struggles. These stories are not ancient fairy tales—they're real, living messages designed to meet us where we are.

Here are a few timeless truths:

- **David and Goliath:** Faith can overcome any giant.

- **The Prodigal Son:** God's love never runs out.

- **The Good Samaritan:** Compassion doesn't discriminate.

- **Job:** Faith in suffering can lead to double restoration.

- **Ruth:** Loyalty and humility bring blessing.

- **Esther:** Courage and obedience change nations.

- **Daniel:** God protects those who honor Him.

- **Joseph:** Forgiveness makes space for destiny.

- **Jonah:** God's mercy is relentless, even when we run.

- **Loaves and Fishes:** God multiplies what we surrender.

Pray This: "Father God, You are my Friend, my Father, and the Creator of all things. I don't always know what to say, but I trust You. Give me discernment, align my life with Your Word, and let Your promises unfold. I surrender my situation (insert here) to You. Thank You for leading me and sending angels to protect me. I declare Your mercy endures forever. In Jesus' name, Amen."

Ask Yourself When Reading Scripture:

- Who is God in this passage?

- Who am I in light of what He says?

- What's the purpose in this moment?

- Can I surrender my goals and use my gifts to glorify Him?

Trina often asked those questions. She longed for her life to reflect God's glory. When she studied the Psalms, especially Psalm 19, something awakened in her:

"The heavens declare the glory of God; the skies proclaim the work of His hands. Day after day they pour forth speech..."

Trina found strength by speaking these verses out loud. They aligned her heart with God's truth. She listened to meditations on Spotify—one called *Abide* became a favorite. A session titled *I Am Secure* reminded her, "You are secure because Jesus has chosen you." That truth settled deep into her spirit.

She resonated with David—not because he was perfect, but because he was real. David made huge mistakes, but his heart always turned back to God. When he sinned, he didn't run away—he repented. And that's what made him a man after God's own heart. God doesn't expect perfection. He longs for repentance, trust, and surrender.

Even in David's failures—like when he pridefully took a census—he chose to fall into God's mercy rather than face punishment by human hands (2 Samuel 24). In Psalm 30:6-7, he reflected, "When I felt secure, I said, 'I will never be shaken.' Lord, when you favored me, you made my mountain stand firm; but when you hid your face, I was dismayed."

Trina learned something vital: everything she had—peace, provision, strength—was from God. It wasn't about her effort. It was about grace.

The Bible is clear: God gives wealth, and He gives wisdom to steward it. He lifts up and brings low, but always with purpose. In Deuteronomy 8:18, "Remember the Lord your God, for it is He who gives you the ability to produce wealth."

Let this sink in:

- "Every good and perfect gift is from above..." (James 1:17)
- "The Lord is their refuge..." (Psalm 14:6)
- "Let it be unto me according to Your Word..."

So many people wonder if they've missed their calling or if God is distant. But He's not. He's drawing near. He's whispering wisdom. He's guiding us through Scripture, through the Holy Spirit, and through our conscience.

Trina understood that nothing was coincidence. God was in every detail. And even when she couldn't see clearly, she trusted that wisdom from heaven would light her next step.

Friend, surrender to God's agenda. Trust in His wisdom. And remember—wisdom isn't just better than rubies. It's the key to the life you were created to live.

The Art of Surrender

If you have had difficult moments in life, there is a way to beat the system with courage. You can pray about it, breathe, and say, believing that no matter what happens to me, it's all in my best interest. This is when things shift. Life happens for you with this mentality. Since nothing is a surprise to God, we must agree that whatever happens to you and I is true for many reasons. To rebirth a new version of you, redirect you, and get you to a better place that you need to be, no matter the outcome, good or bad. In panic, worry, and anxiety, you can manage it with your thoughts of knowing it's happening for a purpose, and you will be able to overcome it since God wants you to learn something from it.

When we ask for our fears to be stilled, our hearts are renewed while we fix our eyes on the Author and Finisher of our faith. Finally, and yet most surely, we will receive some level of encouragement when we look for it. Paul encourages prayer. He knows that the power of God defeats the enemy. Realizing that the exact same power that defeated death, conquered sin, and raised Christ from the dead is the same power present when we pray. This power demolishes principalities that war against us when we call on the Mighty Name of Jesus. Christ is ultimate and supreme, and God has placed all things, from demonic powers to your car payment, under His feet. Big or small, the things that matter to you are the things that matter to God. He is listening, ready and waiting to act on your behalf, with His wisdom, in His time, to bring about the very best in your life to the glory of His great name. I know the more you evoke His power, you will begin to have faith that sees the possibilities where there is no greater power and no greater name to evoke.

"I just need Jesus."

Letting God into your life. Ok, You may have an understanding of how surrender is key. Well, how do you open your heart to receive God into your life? Unless we are willing to achieve something, nothing will be let go in the process. Which means nothing has truly been gained in the end if we don't let go in the process.

We seemingly cannot typically acquire new skins or new levels without being shaped. Like the avocado tree, to have growth we must prune it. We are no different. Trina grew up on her families farm and noticing how many of the plantain and avocado trees need to be cut and pruned for fruit to grow.

Having perseverance in the midst of the cutting is key, as it is a continued effort to receive God in Jesus' infinite grace.

When despite our inadequacy and failures that oppose us mentally through trials and difficulties, we will not be met by an unmerited hand of God.

Every trial we go through is not for us to have victory but for God to show us how He can step in to help us when we lean on him in full dependence. That will deliver us from our despair if we make choices to honor God when we live life expecting to see God in that season of our lives. Every season is about growing in a faith muscle by believing and receiving.

Here is a story where we do not see the reason for difficulties in a man's life, but God redeems His story in such as way after He truly hated God, but God used His story to show how He chose him without his merit.

Ricardo's story started off with a note from His Father telling his Mother to abort Him. He threatened her, saying he would leave her if she didn't abort him. She chose to keep him, and the Father left her in Puerto Rico. The boy's story was heartbreaking because He was sexually abused by his family constantly until His uncle chose to adopt him. Ricky was excited and felt a glimmer of hope when He felt he must have something for him to be wanted. All he longed for was love. His grandma tried to love him, but it wasn't enough. He kept finding himself being abused by his family. They did the best to love him, though. He was sadly in dangerous situations at a very young age of 9. After being sent to America by his family, Ricardo's rejection continued in his aunt's warm home. He struggled to accept love because of the trauma he had endured. He ran away and slept on the streets for 5 months. Then, a blistering cold came, and he went into his aunt's home for warmth. Since he came in and hid in a warm attic where she didn't see him, he thought he could keep coming in without telling her. She one day caught him going up to the attic and called her husband to come and help. They both told her how it can be challenging to recognize and trust when it finally appears in life, which was why they wanted to start having young men who had been in gangs and on the streets so they had a home to rest and heal from longlasting trauma. The conversation of God came up, and He didn't want to stay if God would be a part of it. He chose to stay for 3 months until they opened the home. Then it was delayed because of rain for a month. Ricardo was able to feel the love of family and rest, which continued with helping the boys who were coming in off the streets and needed to heal from trauma. God's redemption and love showed him the importance of understanding and compassion in supporting individuals who have faced such adversities. As in Job 11:18, "You will be confident because there is hope. You will look carefully about and lie down in safety."

In Trina's life she was able to buy an agenda to help her remember there was no need to worry. **The nearer you are to God the more peace you have.**

She heard that story of Ricardo and remembered how there was a story in the story of Hosea where the powerful and sobering narrative of God's enduring love for His people, Isreal, despite their unfaithfulness. Hosea was a prophet in a time of moral decline in Israel. He married Gomer, who was referred to as a promiscuous woman. God instructs Hosea to marry her, knowing she would be unfaithful. Just as Hosea was told she would not be faithful, Gomer was leaving him and engaging in relationships with other men and even descending into prostitution. Hosea continues to love her deeply and is faithful to her because of their vows. Trina was able to see how Ricky's story reminds her of Hosea's story because Hosea was like our God, who is steadfast and loyal. God's reflecting of grace and mercy through Ricky's life gave Ricky the understanding of boundless love, even in the face of shortcomings and sins. When Ricky turned his back on God by saying he hated God, God remained steadfast in being there for him. Then Trina realized, what if it wasn't God's fault that Ricky was born into a family who abused him? What if God didn't want his life to end up on the streets? What if God felt sad that, just like Gomer, he felt filled with shame and guilt for the sins he had committed? Maybe that's why we are just One Prayer away, and God says to not Worry or be Fearful, for The God of the Ages is with us?

After this, she felt a need to focus on Praying More and Worrying Less.

She even received two antique keys to symbolize the keys of faith and belief that opens doors. Thank God for gifts! If you are worrying about something, I must tell you something infinitely amazing! The important news is that God knows about it. He's just wanting to see how you respond. It is very much to grow in relationship with you. The harder it is, the more he wants you to depend on Him wholeheartedly. Whats even more amazing: He wants to deliver you from it. Just be open to share what's going on with him. Let him know, "God, I am feeling lost. I cast all my burdens into your hands because you care for me. You grant me the desires of my heart. As I surrender all to you, help me to always remember that I can let go & Let God. Thank you for the peace of mind. I need it right now." Trina realized any prayer like that gave her peace. She needed to practice giving it to God. Just trusting God with her prayers. Once sent out, it's in God's hand. She needed to let it go. Let him take it. The more specific the prayer, the better. God wants to know exactly how to send his angels. Ask him what territory he has in your life! He does not barge into any rooms without an open door! Is it for healing or dreams to come to pass? We are able to command things boldly and humbly. "Yes and Amen" is for us to know he says Yes to our Amen when it's in alignment with Gods will. How do you know it's in alignment with Gods will? You ask with a thankful heart that HE can do it and praise Him for moving in any way for you! It's about our heart stance. Crying out with true repentance. You can say I don't know about .... But you know.... Father God, What do you want me to pray?.... He will guide you!

Key: "By myself, I can do nothing; I judge only as I hear, and my judgment is just, for I seek not to please myself but him who sent me." —John 5:30

Imagine in a land filled with luscious green pastures there have sheep. If you close your eyes to this just imagine sheep in a pasture. All of a sudden, a voice from the hills saying to the sheep to move along. Next, Hundreds of sheep come out of nowhere in the direction the voice said to go. Just like in John 10:10 when it says. "My sheep listen to my voice & they will follow me." He gives us more than eternal life. Trina could tell that there are real simple whispers that she constantly could feel in her heart. When it didn't make sense, she listened. Much like the sheep she did not understand the reason why she was guided towards a certain hill and not the other. But, she thanked God that he was present enough to tell her and she was wise enough to spend the little time needed to hear His still voice.

Trina had woken up with a voice many times. She was reading a Bible verse when she felt the words jumping out, "I will make a way where there is no way." Then, she felt the need to go to church in Carlsbad. She kept hearing to go pretty much 30 miles away. She figured out why the moment she was cruising on the I-5 when she was singing praises to God. When she was at church, her lead pastor spoke about something she needed to hear in her spirit. This was THE MESSAGE she NEEDED! It was so insane how she could not have gotten such a good message anywhere else. She knew the Voice of God spoke through people, but wow! It was about Samson and his being one of the three people whose name was mentioned through angelic visitation. His life was going to be so incredible. He was set up to be a miracle boy. A lot of things happened, where he almost lost the call of God. His hair was cut, which was his strength. We all have something that is our strength. Is God able to use us if our power is lost? What if the very thing meant to separate us was to be used to take away our power? Our power can be taken away. But God can use us. He plans to bring his plan known after all is said and done.

Committed to Serving God's Agenda

It changes everything when we operate in the belief that our prayers can release heaven's miracles—when we think big, not for our own gain, but to align with His Kingdom agenda. Being obsessed with inspiring hope, lifting others, and seeing lives transformed by faith? That's a life worth living. When we make God's priorities our own, all of heaven backs us. The vision is released. The anointing flows. Miracles manifest.

Surrendering to God's call means saying yes—even when it's hard, even when it costs us. It means becoming teachable, diligent, and open to growth. It's not about perfection but about being willing. It's carrying that posture with you in your everyday life, even while walking down the street.

One beautiful reminder came to Trina while she was walking through Carlsbad. Joy filled her heart as she crossed the street—so much so that someone stopped her and asked, "Why are you so happy?" Without hesitation, she responded, "I go to a great church!" Her answer was genuine, rooted in her love for community and the presence of God.

That spontaneous moment led to divine alignment. The woman she met, Natasha, later came to a church event where a powerful pastor, Rex Crain, spoke prophetically over her life. He declared restoration after 50 years of pain. He said she would meet a kind man who would bless her life and take her on beautiful trips—and he would not be abusive. Every word came to pass. Trina stayed in touch with Natasha and witnessed God's faithfulness firsthand.

Moments like these revealed to Trina the value of spiritual mentorship. Rex mentored leaders at companies like Facebook and beyond. But more than his credentials, it was the Spirit of Truth he carried. Trina believed wholeheartedly—when God offers you a mentor, take the opportunity. Mentorship moved her forward with greater clarity and purpose.

She learned that the miraculous isn't just taught—it's caught. Sometimes, you are called to step into things you feel unqualified for. Sometimes, you must believe you're worthy before you see the reward. She realized saying, "I'll give, travel, or bless others once I'm successful," places our joy on the other side of achievement. But God calls us to live generously and faithfully even in the midst of lack.

Faith rewrites the script.

Trina met a man in the Navy—wise, kind, and clearly sent by God. He invited her into a business opportunity that aligned perfectly with her heart. She could encourage people, walk by faith, and surround herself with mentors who modeled lives of integrity and purpose. For five years, she grew—spiritually, emotionally, and mentally. She learned to filter emotional decisions, build discipline, and trust God more deeply.

But she also realized healing is layered. Beneath the business success was a longing for love and connection. When the time came, she listened to the Lord's prompting and stepped away. It wasn't easy—but obedience never is. Still, she knew: God had something greater. He always does.

And He's calling you too. Are you listening?

When you say yes to God's agenda, miracles begin to unfold. The world doesn't need more comfort—it needs more surrendered hearts.

Let your life be one of them.

The Wind Under MY Sails

Trina knew it had to end.

There was no more wind left in her—no more pretending. The friendship, as beautiful as it was, could no longer continue. Not because he'd hurt her, but because her heart had drifted far past the borders of friendship. She wanted more. She had fallen for him—deeply, truly, unlike anyone before.

She saw the hand of Jesus on his life. She saw potential, purpose, and even glimpses of the man he was becoming. And that made it all the harder. How could she imagine a future without him in it?

Still, she let go.

From a distance, she kept him in prayer. She knew he had a long road ahead. There were things in his life that needed healing, maturing, and surrendering. But she didn't try to control it. Instead, she trusted God. That trust was something she was learning—not just in theory, but in practice.

It was through her connect group and church community that she began to breathe again. They reminded her of something simple, yet profound: *Choose someone who brings life to your future—not confusion to your present.*

It shifted her perspective.

She thought, *What if marriage wasn't about someone who already had it all together—a dream job, polished plans—but someone planted in the church, rooted in growth?*

That kind of man could flourish. That kind of man would grow, because community has a way of pulling the best out of you.

And she realized something else—something freeing:

It's good to be around people who tell you what you **need** to hear, not just what you want. A friend will speak truth; a boss might not.

Still, questions lingered.

The uncertainty made her pause.

How was God going to help her sort through all of this?

She felt like she needed help in every direction. And one thing she knew for sure—she didn't want to settle. Not for a guy who was just charming. Not for someone who turned heads but couldn't lead a heart.

The enemy knew her purpose was significant—and that made her a target. Distractions came easily: beach days, group events, rollerblading on the boardwalk, long workouts that wore out the body but not the questions in her soul.

But even in those moments, she came back to what grounded her: worship.

She remembered the little home church where it all began. The voices, the intimacy, the declarations that stuck with her ever since:

God is Good. God is Great. God is Gracious. God is Glorious.

She carried that with her. And in time, she saw it clearly:

Every season, every person, every joy and heartache had left something behind—a lesson, a truth, a reminder.

She hadn't just lost something when she let go of that friendship. She had made room for what God was preparing next.

One such song that stirred Trina's heart was "God, Turn It Around" by Jon Reddick. The lyrics echoed in the background as she sat at a cozy coffee shop in beautiful Carlsbad:

"All of my hope is in the name of Jesus. Breakthrough will come in the name of Jesus!"

As the song played, Trina sipped her drink and listened to a nearby conversation. A woman at the next table was talking about her dog. "She's a rescue," she said with pride.

Trina smiled politely but couldn't help the thought that followed. *That's wonderful... but sometimes I wonder—did she rescue the dog, or did the dog rescue her?*

It felt like an awful thing to think, especially as a dog lover herself. But today, Trina was struck by something deeper: so many people were simply looking for love, comfort, and companionship.

And when that doesn't come from the One who created us—the One who longs to hear our hearts—we reach for it elsewhere. For some, it's a partner. For others, it's a dog or a cat. Even a bird. And while those bonds are beautiful, Trina wondered: *Are we turning to animals to fill a void only God can satisfy?*

In Colombia, where Trina grew up, dogs were part of life—but not often seen as emotional companions. Her own family dog lived outside, guarding the home, enjoying the natural world. It was hard to imagine then that in other parts of the world, pets were treated like children—kept close at all times, pampered, and spoken to like humans.

Was it really love? Or dependency?

She wasn't trying to be judgmental—just honest. *If someone can't imagine life without their pet, but rarely talks to God,* she thought, *it might be worth reflecting on who's really filling the space in their heart.*

Because the **power of God**—His Spirit—can reach into the deepest corners of our pain and **rescue** us in a way no animal or even human being ever could.

Yes, pets can bring comfort. They can feel like children. Trina even overheard one of the baristas say, "It's like having a child."

Another laughed, "I couldn't do it. It's too much work. I'm too selfish."

And then another sang randomly behind the counter, "Blah, blah, blaaaah," as if mocking the whole idea.

Trina smiled but also felt the weight of what was missing. Our society, for all its progress, often forgets the **power that lies within**—the connection to our Creator.

We breathe, but not with intention.

We move, but not with purpose.

We seek comfort, but not always from the One who offers eternal peace.

She had learned that even *how* we breathe can change our electromagnetic field—science affirms it. And when we breathe with the Spirit of God, something aligns. Peace enters. Fear fades.

But even knowledge isn't enough. You have to **ask.**

You have to **seek.**

You have to **invite Him in.**

Trina wanted others to experience what she had:

That the Spirit of God can teach, comfort, and guide in every situation—big or small. But you have to tap into the identity He already placed within you.

In *Jeremiah 29:13*, God promises:

"You will seek me and find me when you seek me with all your heart."

And in Hebrews 11:6:

"He rewards those who diligently seek Him."

During the pandemic, Trina discovered Graham Cooke's soaking meditations. For two hours a day, she would rest in the presence of God, allowing those words to wash over her. She was already passionate about seeking Him—but those quiet hours made it real. Powerful. Personal.

She recommends you start—even if just five minutes a day. That quiet space can change everything.

Challenge

Lord God, show me who I am in Christ.

Bring the right people into my life to help me walk in truth.

Lead me, guide me, and reveal the purpose you've placed within me.

I want to know who I am—fully and completely—in You.

In Jesus' mighty and powerful name, Amen.

Prayer of Gratitude

Lord God, thank You for who You are and all You've done for me.

Just like David prayed in Psalm 27:4—

"One thing I have asked of the Lord, and that I will seek:

That I may dwell in the house of the Lord all the days of my life,

To gaze upon the beauty of the Lord and to meditate in His temple."

I trust You, Father—the One who placed the stars in the sky and the fish in the sea.

In Jesus' mighty name, Amen.

He Is a God of Provision

We all come to understand God's provision in different ways. For some, it's through witnessing a miracle. For others, it's through daily gratitude—like overcoming financial hardships when there seems to be no way. For Trina, it was both.

She used to believe that if she simply never *thought* about financial trouble, it would never find her. But life has a way of breaking through our illusions. And when it did, God met her there. His Word reminded her:

"I have told you these things, so that in Me you may have peace. In this world, you will have trouble. But take heart! I have overcome the world." — *John 16:33*

It may feel far off when you're in the middle of your struggle, but know this: **you can always pray for help.** He *will* hear you.

Declare this over your life, even when your mind doubts:

"If we know that He hears us—whatever we ask—we know that we have what we asked of Him." — *1 John 5:15*

Trina could testify. She had seen God provide time and again. As a single woman in San Diego, living on less than $45,000 a year for many years, she wasn't sharing to boast—but to point to **God's faithfulness.**

He had been her source. Her sustainer. Her strength.

God wants you to see the victory He's already won for you—over addiction, over depression, over poverty, over every lie the enemy has used to keep you down. He has **commanded a blessing** over your life because His Son took on every curse, including the lie of lack.

One verse Trina clung to was:

"His divine power has given us everything we need for life and godliness through our knowledge of Him who called us by His own glory and goodness." — *2 Peter 1:3 (NIV)*

There is **purpose** in your struggle. It's the proving ground for faith, the space where victory begins.

A Key to Ponder Daily

Dare to dream.

For it is the **choices you make** that will lead you into the *abundant life* God has called you to live.

Trina often noticed how easy it was for married couples to lose connection. What began with romance could become routine. Between full-time jobs, school drop-offs, grocery runs, cooking, and cleaning—just catching a breath felt like a victory. Stress piles up when left unchecked.

That's why she created a simple mental tool called **AGB**—*A Great Blessing.*

Whenever you find it hard to enjoy where you are, remember this:

- **A – Alternative:** Ask yourself: *What's the alternative?* Even if you're cleaning—thank God you have a home, a floor to clean, or a bed to make. Someone else is praying for that very thing.

- **G – Gratefulness:** Gratitude can shift your atmosphere instantly. It's a powerful weapon against stress and heaviness. Pause and thank God, even for the smallest blessings.

- **B – Breathe:** Breathing deeply doesn't just relax you—it literally changes your body. It resets your pituitary gland, realigns your nervous system, and shifts your electromagnetic field. Try it when you feel anxious. Or even when you're filled with joy. Let it anchor you.

Trina knew this truth deeply. She had been building a small business, and every month the pressure to stay afloat was real. It cost nearly $1,000 just to keep things running—with no guarantee she'd make enough for rent, food, gas, or bills.

She turned to the promise in Philippians 4:19:

"And my God will supply all your needs from His glorious riches, which have been given to us in Christ Jesus."

And it was true. Month after month. He provided—just enough. And through that scarcity, a revelation emerged:

When she had nothing, she realized she had everything—in Christ.

We all face choices. And God, in His love, gives us the freedom to choose Him.

That means He's not surprised by your struggle.

Not today.

Not ever.

He is the **Alpha and Omega**, the beginning and the end—outside of time and space.

Nothing catches Him off guard.

So take heart. You are **not a victim** of your circumstances—you are a **victor** through Christ. And when you begin to walk in that truth, you'll start to see Him in all His glory.

From glory to glory.

Take that in.

Sit with it.

Meditate on those moments when the light feels far away.

Even there, **He is with you.**

And He is enough.

You Got the Power

"Life and death are in the power of the tongue…" — *Proverbs 18:21*

We've all heard it: *words have power.* But do we really believe it?

Speaking life—speaking positively over yourself—isn't just a motivational phrase. It's spiritual warfare. It's how we preserve our peace. And peace can be fragile if not protected.

Trina learned this deeply. She realized that when God is the center of your thoughts and words, peace becomes possible—even in chaos.

"You know what I am going to say even before I say it, LORD." — *Psalm 139:4*

That verse wasn't just poetic to her—it was real. God knows it all. He sees your heart, your pain, your motives, your victories. He's never far. So why abandon the very peace you've always longed for?

Stop Striving—Start Trusting

One of Trina's greatest revelations came when she stopped striving. Yes, there's a time to act in faith—but forcing things outside of God's timing leads to stress, not peace.

She remembered what Jesus said in Matthew 6:32:

"Your Heavenly Father knows that you need all these things."

God knows what you need before you ask. He wants to give, not withhold. He operates through **love**, not pressure. So when you find yourself trying to make things happen on your own, take a step back and ask: *Am I trusting Him? Or trying to control it?*

Breakthrough often comes not from *doing more*, but from *being still*.

Faith Unlocks Favor

"Do you disregard the riches of His kindness… not realizing that God's kindness leads you to repentance?" — *Romans 2:4*

When you draw near to Him, a passion grows inside you—a hunger for more of Him. That hunger creates a holy tension: a pull toward the breakthrough you're waiting for, and a peace in trusting that God is at work even when you can't see it.

"God is able to make all grace abound to you… so that you will abound in every good work." — *2 Corinthians 9:8*

You can rest in this: **God cannot fail.**

His mercy and love are not earned—they're gifts. When you walk in faith and love, you're building the foundation for blessing.

Encounters with Grace

Trina experienced this firsthand during a trip to Las Vegas. While it began as a fun getaway, it quickly turned spiritual. She found herself in confusing situations—lost, uncertain, emotionally off balance—but time and again, help came.

Strangers, who she believed were angels in disguise, appeared at just the right time. One of her family members even sensed she'd had spiritual encounters and asked her about it. It confirmed what Trina felt: *She was protected. Set apart. Covered.*

That protection wasn't because she was perfect—it was because of faith. The prayers of her mother. The heritage of belief she carried. The love of a God who rescues and redeems.

Breaking Free from Spiritual Amnesia

Faithlessness creeps in through forgetfulness.

We become like the Israelites—delivered from Egypt but grumbling in the wilderness. Trina recognized the danger of spiritual amnesia: forgetting what God has done, and questioning whether He'll come through again.

"Let all who take refuge in You be glad; let them ever sing for joy… because You defend them." — *Psalm 5:11*

Our posture in hard times reveals our heart. Do we grumble? Or do we trust?

Even in pain, disappointment, or confusion, gratitude is the antidote. It aligns your spirit with Heaven and invites God's presence into your situation.

The Dream and the "Outlaw"

Trina had a dream. In it, she was on a boat, and when she awoke, she saw the word *"Outlaw"* etched on a placard. It stayed with her. At the time, she felt like she was navigating life alone—on a path no one else understood.

Eventually, she was encouraged to write a resentment inventory. As she examined her past, she realized something: she had made inner vows to protect herself, especially from those who loved her most.

One moment stood out—when her mom found out she had self-harmed after being told she couldn't see her friends. Trina had internalized a lie: *that love was conditional, that people couldn't be trusted, that she had to protect herself.*

But it was a misunderstanding. Her parents were trying to protect her, not punish her. She believed a lie, and that lie shaped her reality.

That day, she chose to rewrite the story.

Mindset #30: All Things Are Possible

God keeps His promises.

His Word stands.

You can declare it with authority.

"Let every man praise the Lord who has breath."

"Being fully persuaded that God had the power to do what He had promised." — Romans 4:21

Are you living under the weight of other people's words? Or God's Word?

Let go of bitterness. It poisons the body and soul. Forgive—fully and freely. Picture all your offenses under a rug. That's how God sees you when you come to Him. He doesn't shame you—He cleans you.

Stay in a Bubble of Love

Satan won't stop attacking. But you don't have to be shaken.

"In this world you will have trouble. But take heart! I have overcome the world." — John 16:33

Trina used to tape a note on her closet door: **Do Not Worry.**

Every day, she needed that reminder. Anxiety wasn't just emotional—it was spiritual warfare. She battled fear with faith. She replaced lies with truth. She sang over her soul:

"What a friend we have in Jesus…"

She learned to say:

"Help me, God, to trust You. Help me to be still and know." — *Psalm 46:10*

"The Lord is good to all; His tender mercies are over all His works." — *Psalm 145:9*

He is faithful. He is good. He is the One who breathes new life into brokenness.

Resilience and Mental Toughness

Start here:

Prayer of Power and Peace:

"Thank You, Lord. You know everything.

I want to learn how to hear Your voice.

I come to You in gratitude because You promised to help me—through Your love, Your mercy, and Your Word.

I declare You will continue to provide according to Christ's riches in glory.

I want Your peace, Lord.

As it says in 2 Timothy 1:7, 'You have not given me a spirit of fear but of power, love, and a sound mind.'

I trust You to go before me.

Show me what to do.

I believe that the best days are still ahead.

In Jesus' mighty name, Amen."

Value-Based Learning

The cares of this world can choke the vision God has placed in your heart. But you don't have to carry them—cast your cares on Him, because He truly cares for you.

What may seem impossible—like being healed from terminal cancer—becomes possible when you carry the Word of God in your mouth and heart. *"By His wounds, you have been healed"* (1 Peter 2:24). He bled for you. He is your provider—Jehovah Jireh. So wage the war He has called you to, even if what you see doesn't yet look like victory.

If He did it for others, He can do it for you. Whether it's healing, provision, or even the finances for a home—He's faithful.

Salvation is not just about eternity; it's about transformation now. He has given you the mind of Christ. When you align your thoughts and words with His Word, He aligns your life with His promises. You may feel like you're budding before your time—but God is ready to perform His Word in your life.

Maybe somewhere along the way, you took your eyes off Him. Like Peter, when he saw the waves instead of Jesus, he began to sink. That's what happens when we focus more on the world than on the One who saves us.

Trina loved Peter's story. Introduced to Jesus by his brother Andrew, Peter—though impulsive and bold—became the "rock" upon which Jesus built His Church. He was just like many of us: full of passion, sometimes messy, often trying to prove himself. He was married (1 Corinthians 9:5), and ran a successful fishing business with James and John (Luke 5:10).

Trina could relate. Her performance-driven mindset kept her striving—until Jesus showed her a better way. Like in Luke 5, when Peter had fished all night with nothing to show for it, Jesus stepped into the situation. After all Peter's toiling, Jesus simply said, "Let down your nets." It wasn't about effort—it was about trust.

Jesus was telling him, *"Let that mindset of struggle die. Let Me raise your faith from the unseen into the seen."*

You have access to resurrection power.

Look at what Jesus did in Peter's story. Look at where you are now—not just where you're going, but where you've already come from. Like Peter, Trina wanted to be molded by Jesus, reshaped into the person He always saw her becoming.

Finances Built-in Trust

Trust, in this case, is like a gift box—wrapped with care and tied with a bow. Inside that box, we, whether single or married, can place our finances—entrusting them fully into the hands of God.

He is our provider. And when we honor Him by asking for wisdom in stewarding what He's given us, we step into a daily partnership with Heaven. That is a beautiful form of worship.

Have you ever stopped to think about how He has provided for you since birth? Through every season—childhood, adulthood, and even your daily needs? The same God who feeds the birds and cares for the land is the same One who watches over you.

As it says in Matthew 6:26 (KJV):

"Behold the fowls of the air: for they sow not, neither do they reap, nor gather into barns; yet your heavenly Father feedeth them. Are ye not much better than they?"

The beginning of trust isn't in statistics or probability—it's in the belief that your breakthrough lives in the 1%, not the 99%. That's how Trina lived for over a decade.

What if she could live in San Diego and afford the rent—even without a stable income?

Month after month, Trina personally experienced God's provision. She was never late with rent, even as the cost of living climbed. She came to know this truth deeply:

"The God of the Ages always makes a way."

Even when she didn't have a job, she trusted that her Provider would not fail her. She reminded herself daily:

"Just because I don't have a job doesn't mean God won't find a way to provide."

Trina knew she was deeply loved by God. And when you know that, you begin to see just how far He will go to pursue your heart and rescue your circumstances.

A Key to Ponder Daily:

Trina stayed open to the ways God could bless her.

She would speak words of expectation over her life:

"I am expecting money to come in—effortlessly and consistently—every single day."

During COVID, she had a contract job, renewed every three months. Then came a job at Massage Envy—modest pay, but a grateful heart. Even without government assistance, every bill was paid on time. Every. Single. Time.

God kept showing up.

As the Bible promises:

"God graciously provides exceedingly abundantly beyond all that we ask or think."

(Based on Ephesians 3:20 and taught in Genesis 45:16–28)

According to Bible.org, there are four truths about God's provision:

1. God provides abundantly for all our needs.

2. He cares about every area—material, emotional, and spiritual.

3. He meets us right where we are.

4. His timing and methods are often unexpected—but always perfect.

And as Jeremiah 29:11 declares:

"'For I know the plans I have for you,' declares the Lord, 'plans to prosper you and not to harm you, plans to give you hope and a future.'"

Let your trust be the box you hand over to Him. Put your finances inside, close the lid with faith, and tie it with gratitude.

Then... watch what He does.

He Won't Give You More Than You Can Handle

You've probably heard the phrase, "God won't give you more than you can handle." That's rooted in 1 Corinthians 10:13:

"There hath no temptation taken you but such as is common to man: but God is faithful, who will not suffer you to be tempted above that ye are able; but will with the temptation also make a way to escape, that ye may be able to bear it."

God is faithful. He knows exactly what you can carry—and He also provides a way out when it feels like too much.

Trina knows this personally. She gave up her career—or whatever version of one she had! (Let's be honest—she didn't exactly love being an Administrative Assistant or doing Payroll at hospitals.) Ugh. It drained her, and it never felt like her calling. She barely made enough money to live on, let alone what she dreamed of earning.

Her dreams were of travel, spontaneous coffee shop conversations, encouraging strangers, and spreading joy wherever she went.

But during that long season of waiting, she was being reshaped into someone who *could* wait. She learned to sit with hope, even when the timeline made no sense.

"Rejoice in hope, be patient in tribulation, be constant in prayer." *—Romans 12:12*

As she waited, she kept coming back to God—not to rush Him, but to trust that *He* would open the right door at the right time.

And it wasn't the first door.

After applying for job after job, she walked into a job fair and felt a quiet nudge about a hotel hostess position. Something about that role drew her in— the way the hotel treated its guests with excellence, the way it valued care and service. It clicked.

She got to be her sunshiney, people-loving self. And yes—she also got to "kindly" boss people around! It felt natural. She laughed at how much she resembled Peter in the Bible—impulsive, a little controlling, and very sure of how things *should* be done. (Her excuse? Her parents ran a business—she grew up knowing how to make things happen.)

Still, even this role came with struggles. Her roommate asked her to move out, and money was tight. The family-owned hotel business wasn't easy—regular customers didn't always mean regular pay. She was barely working 40 hours a week.

She prayed constantly. In her quiet time, she heard the Lord whisper to her heart:

"It will all work out."

So she kept going. She rode her bike to work to save gas—especially since her car only took premium fuel. (Of course it did.) Still, she found joy in the small things. She continued meeting with God, morning and night, in her "secret place."

That secret place? A tiny loft in her apartment—technically meant for luggage or storage. But Trina turned it into a prayer room. She knew it was God-ordained.

Though she joked with Him:

"God, I can't keep climbing up here with my Ikea furniture. That shredded wooden table's not going to hold up forever!"

So she went on a mission for a ladder.

Amazon failed her.

But when she checked her storage unit?

There it was. The perfect wooden ladder. Just the right height for her little "loft." ☺

God really does take care of the details.

What's Stopping You?

Trina had been enjoying life in Crown Point, San Diego—one of the most beautiful places to live. But by mid-August, she sensed it was time to move. She put in her two weeks' notice and told her boss. Word spread quickly. To her surprise, the owner of the hotel offered her a chance to stay.

But something deeper stirred in her heart—something wild and green. A vision of the jungle. Again and again, she kept hearing it: **Go to Hawaii.**

Her friends had just moved there, and she desperately needed a break. So, she prayed:

"Lord, I'll go—but the ticket has to be $300 round trip."

And just like that, it happened. A round-trip ticket to Hawaii for $300—**post-COVID and pre-Maui fires**, when prices were normally well over $500. She knew it was a gift from God—another moment shaped in His presence.

Keys to Ponder:

- Ask that your Father would be glorified—in your finances, your decisions, your journey.

- Ask for mercy and grace—for your family and for the nations.

- When you open your mouth in prayer, you don't know what miracle is on the other side.

Then it hit her: *Oh my gosh—I have to move, and I have less than a week!*

And still, she was calm—*chill as a cucumber*—with nowhere to live yet and only a few applications out. But she chose to see it all as a journey. She trusted that God would open the right door. So she enjoyed the hunt.

She had applied everywhere—but was she looking in the *right* places?

That's when Trina learned: her search would only succeed if she searched **with God.**

So she began to write it down, just as it says in Habakkuk 2:2:

"Then the Lord answered me and said, 'Write the vision and engrave it plainly on tablets so that the one who reads it may run.'"

She felt an urgency to record it in what she called her **Book of Miracles**—a place to log God's provision, answers, and growth moments. She highly recommends keeping one. You never know when you'll need to look back and remember.

A Lesson in Identity:

Trina realized how often we attach our identity to what we *do*. One missed devotional. One skipped journal entry. And suddenly we think, "Do I still expect God to show up for me?"

But she learned:

You are capable because He guides you. Not because you perform for Him.

So, she wrote in her Book of Miracles:

"You will find a place near the beach and the bay for $1200."

And guess what? She found it. On Craigslist of all places. She brought a friend to check it out—a **studio one block from the beach, one block from the bay**, right on the edge of the peninsula she had dreamed of living on. $1200.

She signed the lease right before heading to Hawaii for her birthday.

God even confirmed it in a vision:

She saw herself sitting on the bed in that studio, leaning over and praying. Months later, another vision confirmed the price and the timing. The unit was only available for **two months**—and God told her, *"It will work out."*

Little did she know—her grandmother would soon pass away, and she would need to be with her mom in Colombia. The timing? Perfect.

The Pressure to Perform

We live in a world that constantly tells us:

"You need to get it all done."

But what if I told you this?

You have nothing left to prove.

The pressure to complete every task "perfectly and thoughtfully" can be overwhelming. Trina had to shift her mindset:

Doing an excellent job requires wise thinking—and patience.

Step by step. Don't skip steps. Skipped steps lead to breakdowns.

Manage your time.

Delegate when you can.

And learn to manage your anxiety to the best of your ability.

If you don't learn how to manage the stress and anxiety it may distract you from your purpose. You will see Him in the most unimaginable ways when you ask Him for help.

When Overwhelm Hits

We've all felt that way. Trina learned something valuable:

When everything feels like too much—**stop.**

She would pause—go for a walk, sit on her couch, breathe. Then ask: **What's my next step?**

She accepted she would *always* have a long to-do list. That's just life.

Especially if you're aiming for something meaningful.

She learned to lead not with force, but through the quiet strength of communication led by love.

As she listened more and spoke with intention, her confidence began to grow—not in herself alone, but in the One who was shaping her.

She started to see herself—and others—not through the lens of the world, but through the eyes of Jesus, who calls us to become more like Him.

True leadership, she discovered, reflects the heart of Christ: strong yet surrendered, calm yet courageous, steady in thought and grounded in peace.

And isn't that what the Beatitudes invite us into?

To give grace freely, extend mercy without measure, and walk humbly as peacemakers—those who carry heaven's posture into earth's chaos.

Committed to Serving God's Agenda

It changes everything when we operate in the belief that our prayers can release heaven's miracles—when we think big, not for our own gain, but to align with His Kingdom agenda. Being consumed with inspiring hope, lifting others, and seeing lives transformed by faith? That's a life worth living. When we make God's priorities our own, all of heaven backs us. The vision is released. The anointing flows. Miracles manifest.

Surrendering to God's call means saying yes—even when it's hard, even when it costs us. It means becoming teachable, diligent, and open to growth. It's not about perfection, but about a posture of willingness. Carry that heart with you everywhere—even in the simple, ordinary moments of life.

One such moment came to Trina as she was walking through Carlsbad. Joy bubbled up inside her as she crossed a street—so noticeably that someone paused to ask, "Why are you so happy?" With a big smile, she responded, "I go to a great church!" Her words were simple, yet they carried the power of community and the presence of God.

That spontaneous encounter became a divine appointment. The woman, Natasha, later attended a church gathering where a powerful pastor, Rex Crain, spoke prophetically over her life. He declared that after 50 years of difficulty, restoration was coming. He spoke of a loving man who would take her on beautiful trips and never bring harm. And every word came to pass. Trina stayed connected with Natasha and was amazed to see the testimony unfold—exactly as God had spoken.

It was a moment that reminded Trina of the power of mentorship and divine alignment. Rex wasn't just a pastor—he carried a spirit of truth and wisdom. He had mentored leaders at places like Facebook and beyond, but more importantly, he was surrendered to the Holy Spirit. Trina knew: when God offers a mentor, take the invitation. That relationship helped her move forward with clarity and courage.

She began to see that the miraculous isn't always taught—it's caught. Sometimes God asks you to step into something that feels far beyond your capacity. Sometimes He asks you to believe you're worthy before the reward appears. She realized that waiting for "success" before giving or living with joy places her hope in achievement—not in God.

Faith rewrites that story.

Trina eventually met a man in the Navy—someone kind, wise, and clearly God-sent. He introduced her to a business opportunity that aligned perfectly with her gifts. She could encourage others, exercise faith, and surround herself with mentors who lived purpose-filled lives. For five years, she invested deeply—growing spiritually, emotionally, and mentally. She learned how to filter emotional decisions, build discipline, and anchor herself in God's truth.

But she also discovered that healing happens in layers. Underneath the growth and outward success was still a longing for deeper love and partnership.

When the time came, she sensed the Lord calling her to step away from that season. It wasn't easy—but obedience rarely is.

Still, she knew: God had something greater. He always does.

And He's calling you too.

Will you say yes?

When you commit to God's agenda, you begin to see miracles unfold. The world doesn't need more comfort—it needs surrendered hearts. Let yours be one of them.

There Is SO Much More—
Abundantly More

Trina could recall countless moments that unlocked the miraculous. But one stood out above the rest—one that still brings her to tears.

Her father had cancer. And for a long time, he didn't believe that God would speak to someone like him. He assumed God was too distant, too occupied, and surely wouldn't choose someone like Trina to be His messenger.

But Trina believed. She stood in faith for months. And her mom joined her—not just in prayer but in practical obedience. Every morning, for ten months, Trina's mom followed a natural routine to create an alkaline environment in his body—grating frozen lemon into hot water without sugar, first thing each day.

Then, something shifted. One day, her father heard from God. And not long after, he was *healed*. Completely. What doctors had named as a threat to his life became a testimony to God's power.

That healing deepened Trina's expectancy. She began to recognize that faith doesn't operate in isolation. It's fueled by remembrance. She started drawing from past experiences, those moments when God came through. When she couldn't afford a new car after hers was totaled, she didn't spiral. She praised.

She woke up early on Sundays and thanked God for what only *He* could do. She reached out to a trusted friend—someone she hadn't spoken to in a while but felt prompted to contact. He had always been good with financial wisdom, and she knew he was grounded in faith.

What happened next floored her.

After the 10 a.m. church service, standing in the Hertz rental office, her friend said gently, "I am a servant of the Lord. My money is to bless others in need." He paid $700 out of his own pocket so she could have a rental car for the week. Trina was stunned by the generosity—and deeply humbled. He wasn't just helping her—he was preparing to go serve in war-torn Ukraine.

The week passed, and no new rental options opened. For a month, she relied on the kindness of others. Friends offered rides. She took Ubers to work.

She had just signed up to serve on the church welcome team—and the accident had happened that very Sunday.

But still, she trusted.

Then came February 24th. The day she bought her car—a car that matched the vision God had placed on her heart long before. She laughed in awe. She thought she had it all figured out. But then—**BUT GOD.**

He confirmed it, again, on a Sunday. A full-circle moment. A whisper of divine orchestration.

At her church, Pastor Jon Heindrichs teaches about creating a spiritual "Drop Zone"—a time and space where God can pour His truth directly into your life. That season taught Trina just how real and personal God's involvement is. The pastors heard from the Holy Spirit. Her spiritual mother stepped in and prayed powerfully against the enemy's schemes the *very next day* after the accident. Trina believed her quick recovery was no coincidence—it was a direct result of those prayers.

The devil wants chaos, confusion, and exhaustion. But God? He brings *peace*. Even in the waiting.

So she learned to hand over every frustration. Not just theoretically—but practically.

Imagine life as a restaurant. You're the guest, and God is the One waiting to take your order—not to serve *you* in selfishness, but to carry your burdens. Trina was taught to place her emotions, struggles, and questions on a platter—and hand them to the One who could actually do something with them.

Because here's the truth: **we have angels assigned to help us.** *Armies of them. And they are waiting for you to believe in their assignment. "Give all your worries and cares to God, for He cares about you." — 1 Peter 5:7*

Scripture tells us again and again—when we obey, we live. —Nehemiah 9:29

Above Inspiration

Trina also remembered a powerful speech by actor Chris Pratt at an award ceremony. His words stuck with her—and still do:

"God is real.

God loves you.

God wants the best for you.

Believe that. I do.

If you're strong, be a protector.

If you're smart, be a humble influencer.

Strength and intelligence are weapons. Don't wield them against the weak.

You have a soul. Be careful with it.

Learn to pray. It's easy and it's good for your soul.

Nobody is perfect.

You are imperfect. You always will be, but there is a powerful force in that.

God designed you that way.

If you're willing to accept that, you'll understand grace.

Grace is a gift. Don't take it for granted."

Those words echoed a truth Trina had come to live by:

There is *so much more* God wants to give you.

Abundantly more.

You just have to say yes.

Step One Is Choices: Seeing with the Eyes of Faith

The most important truth to grasp is this: when you invite God in, He will meet you on the journey. He'll give you ideas, whispers of wisdom, and divine strategy to renew your faith and align your steps with His. As Romans 12:2 reminds us, *"Do not conform to the pattern of this world, but be transformed by the renewing of your mind. Then you will be able to test and approve what God's will is—His good, pleasing and perfect will."*

Psalm 119:78-81 beautifully echoes this heart posture: *"May the arrogant be put to shame for wronging me without cause; but I will meditate on your precepts... May those who fear you turn to me, those who understand your precepts."* Precepts—divine principles of truth—guide our decisions and actions when we submit to His will.

Choosing rightly begins with surrender. It means saying "yes" to what stretches you. It means trusting that even the tears, the trials, and the tension can bring about a harvest. Trina once clung to Psalm 119:82, *"My eyes fail, looking for your promise; I say, 'When will you comfort me?'"* In seasons of deep uncertainty, she learned that wise counsel matters. She surrounded herself with mentors who had the fruit she desired. One, in particular, advised her to align with those who inspired ambition and faith.

One specific decision stands out—choosing not to go to a bar alone anymore. It had once felt harmless, even glamorous. She remembered walking into a gorgeous venue and being stunned when five GQ-worthy men walked in. But that moment was a turning point. She drew a line. Her heart was worth protecting.

Faith means seeing what you can't yet touch. It's the substance of what you hope for—and the evidence of what your spirit knows to be true. If we don't practice faith, we'll miss the miracle. Trina often declared: *"I don't want just a good life—I want a God life."* His desires are far greater than we can imagine.

She recalled a couple from her small group. They were convinced they'd move to Denver. All signs pointed that way—until God nudged them to consider Idaho. It made no sense... but in prayer, they asked for confirmation.

The next day, it came. In hindsight, they saw how God had orchestrated everything far better than they could have planned.

That's the thing—God sees what we can't. He knows the people, places, and moments that will shape our destiny. His top priority is not where we live or what we do, but *who we are becoming*. When Trina returned to San Diego after spending time with her mother following the loss of her grandmother, she felt behind. Like she was starting over. But in prayer, God whispered, *"This is a training season. You're learning what you'll one day teach."*

That changed everything.

Daily encounters with God became her anchor. Even five minutes set aside in quietness made a difference. Every time she put others first—every time she chose service over self—God showed up in ways she couldn't have orchestrated. The world says, "Take care of yourself first." But God says, "Seek first My Kingdom, and all these things will be added to you."

In her hardest seasons, God gave her answers, clarity, and peace. He reminded her: *"My love is your strength. I am your portion. I am enough."*

In 1 Peter 5:7 it says, "Cast your anxiety on Him because He cares for you." That truth became her anthem.

Trina was in the thick of it when writing this book. Life felt like a storm, but God's voice calmed the waves. Her job required full reliance on Him—there were no safety nets, no backup plans. Rent was rising, and her income didn't match. Her dependence wasn't just spiritual—it was practical. Every dollar, every open door, every moment of peace came from Him.

Still, she pressed in. She created space for God—literally. Her "upper room" was a little space above her closet, and every morning, she would climb up with a cup of Earl Grey and simply sit. Sometimes for five minutes. Sometimes longer. It didn't matter. That time was sacred. That was her altar.

After reading *Draw the Circle by Mark Batterson*, she embraced 40 days of simply listening. It transformed her. The clutter in her heart fell away. The desire for trivial things disappeared. All she wanted was Him.

One morning, He spoke clearly: *"It will all work out perfectly."* And just like that, peace settled deep in her soul. It didn't change her circumstances right away—but it changed *her*.

The final test came when she needed to explain her work while searching for a new place to live. She wrestled even in her sleep. But prayer changed everything.

Here's what happened next:

Trina surrendered.

She prayed.

She waited.

And heaven responded.

Appointments, resources, conversations—everything aligned. Not just with her desire, but with *His will*. Because she had shifted from praying *for* something to praying *through* something—so that His purposes could shine.

That's where the power is.

When you lay down your timeline, your logic, and your "shoulds"... and say,

"Not my will, but Yours be done."

Then heaven moves.

The more Trina let go, the more she received what her soul *actually* longed for.

God's best.

The kind of trust that moves mountains. The kind of peace that quiets storms.

And friend, it's available to *you*, too.

All you have to do is ask. Try praying this:

"Father God, thank You for all You are doing right now. I know You care deeply for me. I am not forsaken. Please guide me in this situation. I trust You with my needs. I invite the Holy Spirit to lead me into truth, peace, and joy. In Jesus' mighty and powerful name and through the power of the Holy Spirit. Amen."

He Will Never Fail

Trusting in a God who truly loves and cares for you is the beginning of a life marked by peace, assurance, and miracles. When you welcome Him into your life—not out of fear, but out of faith—you begin to witness just how faithful He truly is. And He *will* show up for you in personal, undeniable ways, simply to reveal that He is with you. Always. His heart longs to lead you into His best for your life.

As Trina continued writing this book, she realized something powerful: God's desires for her life were far better than anything she could come up with on her own. And the beauty of this truth? It came through real, practical steps she took in her everyday life—steps she now shares with you so you can apply them, too.

One of those moments was during a season of housing transition, when the question of where to live became incredibly overwhelming. Trina felt like she had to tell everyone, almost as if she needed to fix it herself. But deep down, she heard her spirit whisper: *"Just trust God."*

She remembered Proverbs 3:5-6: *"Trust in the Lord with all your heart and lean not on your own understanding; in all your ways submit to Him, and He will make your paths straight."*

Each day, she would ask God to lead her steps. And when she felt prompted to reach out to someone or follow up on a conversation, she did. She didn't force things, but remained open and obedient. Miraculously, those nudges were always *right on time*. She didn't have to beg or plead—just be available to hear and respond.

God says, "Cast all your anxiety on Me, because I care for you." —1 Peter 5:7 And *"Do not worry about tomorrow, for tomorrow will worry about itself."* —Matthew 6:34

Another step was simple diligence. People around her began suggesting resources, connections, and places to check out. And instead of giving in to discouragement, she kept moving forward. Scripture confirmed this truth: "The hand of the diligent makes rich." (Proverbs 10:4) and "The soul of the sluggard craves and gets nothing, while the soul of the diligent is richly supplied." (Proverbs 13:4)

One day, she drove far out to view an affordable place. Though uncertain, she felt peace—because she had prayed first. God had reminded her, *"I will give you the desires of your heart."* So she remained open, willing to act and respond in faith.

Here's the thing: sometimes, the process itself is the miracle. It teaches us how to respond *when* life gets hard. And if you're wondering whether God sees you in your situation right now—yes, He does. You have a loving Father who *never* stops fighting for you, even when you're too weary to fight for yourself.

Trina found herself clinging to this truth: *Every word God speaks is a promise.* His love is relentless, deeper and more complete than anything or anyone. No earthly relationship could ever compare to the love of your Creator.

When she had spoken to several potential roommates and was still unsure, she took another intentional step: she wrote down exactly what she hoped for. She journaled. She prayed. She sought God—not just for provision, but for peace. She wanted His will above all.

It was the day before her trip out of town, right before her move. That morning, she returned to her prayer closet and simply sat with the Lord. She rewrote her desires with specificity and childlike faith, remembering Philippians 4:6: *"Do not be anxious about anything, but in every situation, by prayer and petition, with thanksgiving, present your requests to God."*

And that's what she did—she handed it all over.

In those quiet moments, God reminded her to look back and *remember*. Reflecting on past faithfulness awakened hope for her future. There were so many times He had come through for her. Why would this be any different?

People often say, *"It always works out in the end,"* but it means so much more when you've *seen* God show up for you over and over again. That belief begins to transform your subconscious—it shifts your mindset from fear to faith.

Even when her mother expressed worry, Trina held on to a different vision. One filled with peace. One led by God. She imagined herself living in a new space, filled with light, love, and tranquility. She envisioned what God had already prepared for her.

And you know what? That vision gave her something to hope for. Something to *walk toward* in faith.

She Envisioned...

Staying aligned with God led Trina exactly where she needed to go—not just physically, but in her soul. It wasn't a sudden arrival, but a slow unfolding, shaped by choices. She chose intimacy over interruption. Prayer over pressure. Stillness over striving. She chose *Him*.

In that sacred space of communion, vision began to bloom.

She started to *see* things differently—through the lens of faith.

She pictured her new home, full of peace and light.

She envisioned herself receiving blessings she never thought she could have.

She imagined what it might feel like to be celebrated, chosen, and free.

There were many moments she could've been pulled off course. Life, with all its noise and demands, beckoned her to be distracted. But she stayed rooted. Anchored in quiet trust.

She began to understand that envisioning wasn't just imagination—it was spiritual alignment. A holy posture of surrender. She positioned herself, not only in prayer, but in expectation. *Not frantic, but faithful. Not striving, but still.*

She sat in the presence of God...

...not just quiet, but open.

...not just waiting, but *believing*.

...not just hoping, but *trusting*.

And in that posture, her spirit softened. Her heart was ready to receive.

Healing Through Presence

During one of those quiet Thursday mornings with her women's prayer group, a dear friend named Tammy gently offered words that landed in Trina's heart like seed:

"Your triggers can be healed through time with God."

It sounded simple. But it carried the weight of wisdom.

Trina began to press in—deeply, intentionally.

She made time.

She got honest.

She sat still.

And in that sacred stillness, she invited God into every fractured place.

It wasn't always easy. The wounds she carried weren't just surface-level. Some were rooted in childhood—buried beneath years of silence, masked by independence, softened by success. But God saw them all. And He wasn't afraid of any of it.

At first, the stillness was uncomfortable.

It exposed her need.

It revealed her wounds.

But it also welcomed her healing.

So she adjusted her rhythms. She woke up before the noise of the world could steal her peace. She carved out space—time that was *His*. Time that wasn't rushed or filled with performance. Just presence. Just honesty.

This became her holy appointment. A meeting place between the broken and the Divine.

No longer was she running from herself. She was running *to* Him.

And He began to speak.

His voice wasn't loud, but it was unmistakable.

His presence wasn't flashy, but it was transforming.

And His love—it didn't just comfort.

It healed.

Trina realized something profound in that season:

Healing doesn't always start with fixing.

It starts with *feeling*.

It starts with *sitting*.

It starts with *letting God in*.

And in His presence, the pain began to unravel.

The lies began to lose power.

The heart began to hope again.

She envisioned a future shaped not by fear or past wounds, but by *wholeness*.

She saw herself walking in freedom.

She began to believe again.

And the vision God gave her... became her new reality.

Source of Strength

There were moments in Trina's life when she was desperate for direction—but it didn't come the way she expected.

She didn't need more instructions.

She needed *intimacy*.

She didn't need more steps to follow.

She needed to be *fed*.

Strength, she discovered, is not summoned by sheer effort. It is *received*—when we come to God empty and let Him fill us with peace, with love, and with the power of His Spirit.

Jesus, too, was first *filled* by the Spirit before He was *led* by the Spirit. And yet, many of us try to be led without ever being fed. We hunger for answers but miss the nourishment that sustains us. God doesn't just want to tell us what to do—He wants to strengthen our *hearts* with His presence.

There is *more joy* available than we know—more than answers, more than outcomes. Joy is found in devotion, not desperation. And strength is found in His presence, not in our striving.

Trina came to realize:

God wasn't just going to "do it for her."

He wanted to *do it with her*.

He longed to collaborate with her heart.

But she had to step into it.

She had to *choose* it.

Do you want to be financially well? Spiritually whole? Emotionally steady?

Then you must begin by choosing it—choosing to believe that what God has for you is already yours... if you're willing to align with Him.

We often want the *outcome* without the *offering*.

But growth, freedom, and peace have a price: surrender.

Surrender is the action that unlocks spiritual strength.

And trusting God—especially when we're wrestling with limiting beliefs—becomes the daily rhythm that forms endurance, equips us to grow, and gives us strength to endure the next battle.

A Real God for Real Life

God doesn't want distant followers.

He wants *intimate friendship*.

He desires to *walk* with us, to *whisper* to us, to *build us up* with words that help us overcome the very real struggles we face.

Trina remembered the countless times she broke down in her car. In shambles. Overwhelmed.

And yet... there, in the quiet, she would cry out:

"God, I know You can help me do this..."

The doubts didn't disappear instantly. Sometimes, they even grew louder. But she learned that *faith* isn't always about silence from the storm. It's about *presence in the storm.*

Even when there wasn't an audible word from Heaven.

Even when others said, "Just pray about it," and that felt too simple.

She still believed.

She shifted her energy—not by forcing positivity, but by anchoring in *truth.*

"I may not know how this will work out, but I know Who holds me."

Let the Seed Grow

Not every day brought clarity. But every day could bring connection.

What she needed most wasn't just an answer. It was a Word. A verse. A promise. That would be the seed. And in time, seeds grow into something beautiful. Something life-giving. Something *eternal.*

Friend, prepare your heart.

Let Him in.

Welcome Him—not just in your quiet time, but in your chaos.

Not just in your wins, but in your weakness.

Let Him be your source of strength.

And as you do, let this truth wrap around your soul:

"For You created my inmost being;

You knit me together in my mother's womb.

I praise You because I am fearfully and wonderfully made;

Your works are wonderful, I know that full well." — Psalm 139:13–14

You were made for this connection.

And He will always be your strength—your steady, unfailing, Spirit-filled source of hope.

Pro-pulsion!

As you've seen throughout this book, Trina's life has been marked by one steady theme: communion with God. It's what sustained her. Carried her. Transformed her.

Through countless life transitions, she learned this truth—her life was never just about work. It was about something *greater*.

At a pivotal crossroads, she began to ask herself:

Who am I really living for?

What has God gifted me with?

And how can I use everything I've walked through to bless others?

She didn't always have the answers. But she had a pen. And she had faith.

Waking Up to God's Voice

Around 2015, two years into her walk with God, Trina had already been journaling regularly—asking Him questions and patiently listening for His response.

Then one night, everything shifted.

She woke up with an itch—so intense she couldn't sleep. As she sat up, her eyes were drawn to a pen. Something stirred in her spirit. She picked it up, grabbed her notebook, and began to write.

The words flowed.

They weren't from her.

They were from Him.

In that quiet encounter, God poured direction onto the page—showing her what step to take next, reassuring her He was near, and speaking into her future with clarity and love.

A Squid and the Power of Propulsion

During one of her prayer times, God gave her a vivid illustration: the **Squid**.

She realized how, when under pressure, the Squid doesn't panic—it propels.

It doesn't flail around.

It doesn't retreat.

Instead, it takes in water, builds pressure, and then—**pushes it out with force**, launching itself into motion.

Propulsion. That was the word God whispered.

Trina felt it in her spirit: *This is what I want to do with you.*

Take in My Word.

Take in My Spirit.

And then—when the moment is right—launch forward in supernatural momentum.

That's how God works. He fills us in private so He can propel us in purpose.

A Divine Appointment Named Berta

Some time later, Trina met an extraordinary woman named Berta—an 80-year-old who had been journaling to God for more than 50 years.

Their meeting wasn't random. It was *divine.*

Trina was in Colombia visiting her parents, and through an unusual series of events involving a neighboring farm owner, Berta was brought to her.

Trina's mom—struck by the similarity between them—told her, *"Berta is just like you."*

Indeed, Berta's heart mirrored Trina's. She, too, was deeply surrendered to God.

Though Berta had never married, she had lived a full, joyful life with a rich banking career. But in prayer, she would cry out, *"Lord, You've given me everything. I want nothing—because I have You."*

At that point in her life, Trina also longed to be married. And yet, hearing Berta's story deeply encouraged her: she could trust God fully, with everything, even her deepest desires.

Living on Purpose in the Unknown

For Trina, Berta became a confirmation—living proof that God sees, leads, and provides.

At the time, Trina's parents couldn't see the purpose in her journey. She had left her career, had no stable job, and didn't even have a set place to live.

But God saw it all. He was writing a bigger story.

And He sent Berta as a messenger.

Berta had been fasting for two months and never went out at night. But when she visited Trina's family farm, Bethlehem, she invited them into her home. It was an invitation not just to a house, but into God's perspective.

Letting Go of Control

Through their friendship, Trina came to a deeper realization: Her life wasn't hers to control.

Every time things didn't work out the way she planned, it was a divine redirection.

God's timing.

God's hand.

God's plan.

Berta affirmed this with her life. She lived the same way: surrendered, faith-filled, and constantly trusting.

Trina stopped trying to protect herself through her own willpower.

She stopped fearing failure.

She started saying, *"Lord, let them see my life and say, 'How? Wow!'"*

And Berta? She had prayed that very same prayer.

The "Upper Room" and a New Identity

Back in San Diego, after ten years of following God's lead, Trina's circumstances still looked uncertain.

Her roommate had asked her to move out. Her job as a hostess—one she loved for its connection to people—was ending. Her parents were worried. It looked like she had "nothing to show" for her time.

But heaven had a different view.

What others called loss, God called preparation.

And in her prayer closet—her "upper room"—she continued to seek His voice.

Even as prestigious opportunities and beautiful views faded, even as titles were stripped away like old garments, Trina discovered something eternal:

Her identity wasn't in what she did.

It was in who she was.

She let go of chasing status and embraced servanthood.

She chose to live with a heart that said, *"Nothing is above me. Nothing is beneath me."*

And in that humility, she was propelled—not backward, but forward.

By His Spirit.

By His grace.

By His calling.

Father God,

I love that I get to experience how deeply You love me—unconditionally, faithfully, and more completely than anyone on Earth ever could. You long for me to share my life with You, and in doing so, You continually show me how You provide, protect, and guide me.

To know I am loved by You is the greatest feeling in the world. Help me to reflect that love—to be a light in this world, allowing You to shine through me as I pray for others without condition or limit.

In Jesus' mighty and powerful name, and through the Spirit that lives within me—In Jesus' Mighty and powerful Name and through the power of the Holy Spirit.

Amen.

A Yielded Heart Prays for Others

A heart that is yielded to God—one seeking its identity in Him—is open to receiving all that He has prepared. He alone knows what is best, and His desires for us far exceed our own.

There was once a woman who struggled deeply with disappointment in her marriage. She had believed her husband would be the answer to her prayers—a man of strength, faith, and kindness. But instead, she found herself battling resentment and unmet expectations. It seemed like everything she dreamed of was just out of reach.

For years, she wrestled with the Lord about why things didn't turn out the way she'd hoped. But in time, something shifted. She stopped asking God to change her husband and began asking Him to change her heart. She prayed daily, often with a trusted prayer partner, choosing to surrender rather than strive. She brought her pain to the Lord and trusted Him to do what she could not.

One day, after a particularly tearful prayer, she heard the Lord whisper, *"I see you. I'm working in places you cannot see."* She didn't know it then, but that moment of surrender would become the turning point.

Over the following year, God began softening her husband's heart. He started joining her at church, reading scripture with her at breakfast, and even praying over her before bed. One day, he surprised her with a letter—handwritten, heartfelt, and holy—repenting for years of emotional distance and asking her to begin again, this time with God at the center.

That was the start of their *God-sized ending*—a marriage reborn not by effort alone, but by divine intervention. Today, they minister to other couples and share how prayer, patience, and surrender truly change everything.

This is the fruit of a yielded heart.

That's why prayer partners are such a gift. When we pray in unity, something powerful happens. Jesus said, *"For where two or three gather in my name, there am I with them."* (Matthew 18:20). When we come into agreement with others in prayer—even for people we don't know personally—we are taking part in a testimony that is forming.

Jesus also declared in Matthew 21:22, *"If you believe, you will receive whatever you ask for in prayer."* We may not always receive what we imagined, but we receive what is needed, what is good, and what is in alignment with Heaven. Prayer draws us into the purposes God has designed specifically for our lives.

This is how Trina navigated many of her hardest seasons: through prayer and community. When she joined hands with fellow believers, Heaven moved. She found peace, clarity, and assurance that she wasn't walking alone.

There is great comfort in surrender. When we lay our burdens before God, they are not ignored—they are handled. As Matthew 11:30 reminds us, *"His yoke is easy, and His burden is light."* We don't need to carry the weight alone. He already bore it for us. And He has overcome the world.

One Friday night, Trina longed to spend time with friends. Her car was in the shop—damaged from an incident that caused all the airbags to deploy. The disappointment was real. She felt stuck and left out, wondering why things seemed to go wrong just when she needed a break.

But instead of spiraling into frustration, she stayed home and turned to God. She tuned into a message from Graham Cooke that pierced her heart: **"Every situation is meant to bring us closer to Jesus."**

She sat still. *What if that were true?* What if this wasn't just bad luck—but a setup for something greater?

As she let the words sink in, she also remembered the promise of John 10:10, *"Jesus came to give us life, and life more abundantly."* That night, she chose to believe that—even this—was under God's care.

She began praying, *"God, I know You will make all things right."* Her faith wasn't just wishful—it was rooted in the Word. In **1 Peter 5:10-11**, it says,

"After you have suffered a little while, the God of all grace... will Himself restore you and make you strong, firm, and steadfast."

And in **Romans 8:28**, she clung to the truth that,

"All things work together for the good of those who love God and are called according to His purpose."

She even spoke out loud the words of **Isaiah 45:2**,

"I will go before you and make the crooked places straight."

She declared them with conviction, trusting that where there seemed to be no way, God was already preparing one.

And then... the miracle happened.

Within a few days, Trina received a check—unexpected and entirely divine. **$3,900.** A reimbursement from a previous matter that had long been forgotten. But not by God.

The exact timing, the exact amount—it wasn't random. It was a signature from Heaven.

She wept.

Not just because of the money, but because of the message: *"I see you. I hear you. I make all things right."*

It was God's provision wrapped in His love.

This is what it looks like when we surround our problems with His presence. When we surrender our plans and believe that God is working—especially when we don't see how.

The Mother of Our Lord Jesus Christ

Let us speak of those whom God has chosen as vessels of His grace and power. Chief among them is our Savior Jesus Christ, the divine Intercessor. But let us not overlook the tender strength of the Virgin Mary—Mother of our Lord, and a heavenly intermediary of great love and light.

Trina had a profound moment of connection when her grandmother passed away and she spent a month with family. In that sacred time, the light of Mary was undeniable. Mary loves us. She longs to fill us with a radiant light—a light that draws us closer to the heart of God. Even those who do not yet understand her role or seek her intercession are not forgotten. Her love remains. That light still lives within us, illuminating the path toward deeper intimacy with the Holy Spirit.

It is this light that transforms us. It is the lamp to our feet and the guide for our steps. It is the Spirit's gift in us, enabling us to walk as children of the light and do the works that Jesus said we would do—"greater works," as He promised in John 14:12.

Mary's life is marked by intercession. From the wedding at Cana to her presence at the cross, she continually said yes to God's will and stood in the gap for others. Our devotion to Mary is not worship—it is reverence, like introducing someone we deeply love to our own mother. It's a holy relationship, one rooted in trust and comfort.

When we "pray" to Mary, we're simply asking her to pray with us, the way we would ask a faithful friend or spiritual mentor. As we recite the Hail Mary, we echo the words of Scripture—the angel Gabriel's greeting and Elizabeth's blessing:

"Hail, Mary, full of grace, the Lord is with you!" —*Luke 1:28*

"Blessed are you among women, and blessed is the fruit of your womb." —*Luke 1:42*

God chooses to move through people. He always has. Jesus said, "Go and make disciples of all nations," (Matthew 28:19) not by force or spectacle, but through loving relationships and the wisdom of the faithful. Proverbs 22 reminds us to "pay attention to the sayings of the wise" and keep their counsel close to heart. For it is through this guidance that we learn to trust in the Lord.

God also speaks through friends, mentors, and spiritual companions—those who, like Mary, carry wisdom and intercede for others. Proverbs 11:14 reminds us, **"Where there is no guidance, a people falls, but in an abundance of counselors there is safety."**

Prayer

God, You are my Provider and Protector. I trust that You are preparing the way for me—even when I cannot see it. Thank You for placing wise counselors in my life, and for sending Your Holy Spirit to comfort, guide, and empower me. I trust in Your timing and Your plan, even when I walk through valleys of uncertainty. You have chosen me. I choose You back. May I forever walk in Your presence, covered by Your grace, and led by Your truth. In Jesus' Mighty and powerful Name and through the power of the Holy Spirit, Amen.

Angels of War: Justified Living with That Hope

As you read this chapter, may your heart encounter a love unlike any other—a love that is constant, pure, and powerful. May you come to know your God not only as Creator of all things, but as the Author of your story, the Great Counselor, Redeemer, Mighty Protector, and the Lover of your soul. He is the One who restores what has been broken, heals what has been hidden, and provides what we cannot even bring ourselves to ask for. He knows your deepest needs and longings. And He is faithful.

Life is a journey filled with choices—some of them stretch our faith, while others bring us to our knees. There are moments that feel too heavy, too unfair. Moments when nothing makes sense. Perhaps someone we trusted deeply has let us down. Maybe we've endured heartbreak, confusion, or seasons of waiting that felt endless.

But even here, God is at work.

Trina came to realize that trust wasn't a one-time decision. It was daily. Hourly. It meant surrendering the fear of disappointment in exchange for the hope of restoration. It meant releasing the need to control outcomes in order to receive divine peace. She learned that God wasn't asking for perfection—but permission. Permission to step in and be her strength. To redeem every disappointment. To breathe life into the parts of her story she thought were beyond repair.

Hebrews 12:27 speaks to this: *"The words 'once more' indicate the removal of what can be shaken—that is, created things—so that what cannot be shaken may remain."* What a promise. That God is always refining, always purifying, until only the eternal and unshakable remain.

As Trina let go of lesser things—resentments, fears, distractions—she made room for more of God. She saw clearly: the less clutter in her heart, the more space for divine presence. Had she been given everything she once wanted—more time, more resources, more control—without His guidance, it would not have carried the eternal impact she longed for.

She began to ask God boldly, listening more deeply, trusting more freely. And in time, she could sense what He desired for her life. That clarity only came through surrender. Through waiting. Through hope.

She discovered that pain, while uncomfortable, was not without purpose. Pain refined her. It taught her compassion. It gave her wisdom. It led her to prayer. And those prayers? They were not empty words—they were declarations of faith. Anchors in the storm. Seeds that would bear fruit in due time.

She chose to believe:

- *I will recover.*

- *I will bounce back.*

- *The best is yet to come.*

- *Blessings are on the way.*

- *What's coming next will cause me to rejoice.*

Because that's the kind of God she served. The kind who turns mourning into dancing. The kind who brings beauty from ashes. The kind who sends angels of war to defend His beloved ones and who empowers us to live with justified hope.

And you, too, can walk in this hope.

Make decisions that reflect your faith, not your fear. Ask boldly. Trust deeply. Believe that even in perilous times, God is not absent—He is present. And His promises? They will not return void. Your identity, formed in the furnace of trust, will carry you forward into everything He has prepared for you.

The battle may be intense—but you are not alone. The angels of war fight on your behalf. Heaven is backing you. So rise up, not in your own strength, but in the strength of the One who has already overcome.

Challenges and Tests

As human beings, we are not programmed like robots to automatically follow a path of faith. We've been given the gift of free will—the ability to choose, to trust, to believe. And that's what makes our journey with God so precious. Choosing to trust Him, especially in hardship, reveals a strength that only faith can produce.

Every challenge we face becomes an invitation. An invitation to stand firm. To take a stance not just with our words, but with our attitude, our thoughts, and our hearts aligned with God's truth. We are reminded throughout Scripture that it's not our strength that wins battles—but our reliance on Him.

Think of the people of the Bible: Esther, who risked her life to stand for her people. Joseph, who waited through betrayal and prison to see the dream fulfilled. David, who faced a giant not with armor but with faith. They had one thing in common—they trusted a God who sees beyond the challenge into the victory.

Faith becomes our training ground.

When you understand the power of faith in Jesus—your doubts lose their grip. Because you're no longer basing your trust on outcomes, but on the One who holds every outcome in His hands.

Trina came to understand this deeply. There was a time when she thought certain people in her life would never disappoint her. Friends who seemed trustworthy. Mentors she looked up to. Even relationships that felt like forever.

But life has a way of shaking our foundations. People change. Circumstances shift. Trust is tested.

She learned that no one on earth can carry the weight of being your peace. That's a role only God can fulfill. When someone would say, "I don't know what I'd do without you," it sounded loving—but deep down, Trina knew it placed human affection above divine sufficiency.

Everything we have—our health, our homes, our resources, even our relationships—is a gift from God. And when we anchor ourselves in Him, we can weather the storms of loss, betrayal, or uncertainty without losing our peace.

A Story of Faith Through Disappointment

There was a season when Trina was deeply let down by someone she trusted. She had prayed with them, laughed with them, confided in them. When things shifted and that person turned away, the hurt was sharp. It felt like rejection. Like failure.

She brought it to God—raw, unfiltered. And in prayer, she heard a gentle whisper: *"They were never meant to stay forever. I allowed them for a season, but I am the One who remains."*

That moment became a turning point.

Trina began to see that **even our disappointments are allowed by God to refine us.** To strip away misplaced attachments. To teach us how to be rooted in Christ, not in comfort. Not in people. Not in outcomes.

David Diga Hernandez once said that before God blesses you, He will give you three tests. And Trina started to recognize these tests—not as punishments, but as preparation. The loneliness? A test of identity. The financial lack? A test of provision. The betrayal? A test of forgiveness and trust.

She realized that **some people are not meant to go with you to your next level.** And that's okay. Promotion often requires separation. Not to punish, but to protect what God is building in you.

Hebrews 12:27 says:

"The words 'once more' indicate the removal of what can be shaken—that is, created things—so that what cannot be shaken may remain."

This is the heart of every test: to reveal what cannot be shaken. And what remains? Faith. Hope. Trust. Love. Jesus.

So friend, if you're facing disappointment or loss, know this:

You're not being abandoned.

You're being refined.

You're not being punished.

You're being positioned.

God's tests are not to break you—but to build in you an unshakable foundation. When everything else is stripped away, may He be the One who remains at the center.

And in that place, you'll find peace like no other.

Affiliations Eclipsed by Glory

Trina had always known there was something different about her. She carried a quiet conviction that her life was not meant to blend in, but to stand apart—not for glory, but for God.

She wasn't driven by selfish ambition or a need for status. She longed for meaningful connection, for marriage rooted in purpose, and a life spent pouring into others. Her mother had taught her from a young age to serve, to notice the needs of others, and to respond with compassion. Trina took those lessons to heart. She found joy in acts of kindness and fulfillment in giving even when it cost her.

She wasn't interested in dating just for fun. She dreamed of love with intention—of a husband who would cherish her as God intended. Justice mattered to her deeply—not just fairness in society, but integrity in her relationships. She wanted to be a woman who didn't lie, cheat, or manipulate, and who still offered mercy when it was hard to do so.

One day, she was working out with a military trainer. He admired her strength but grew frustrated by her boundaries. When she didn't accept his invitation to spend time outside their training sessions, he scoffed and called her "impossible." The words lodged in her heart, making her question if maybe she was too much.

But God stepped in.

He reminded her of the truth: she wasn't impossible—she was intentional. She was *set apart*. And one day, a man would not only understand her heart but pursue it with humility and purpose. The lies that tried to attach themselves to her identity began to lose their grip as she reclaimed who God said she was.

This wasn't about rejection—it was about refinement.

Trina often meditated on Micah 6:8, which anchored her through moments of confusion and transition:

"He has shown you, O mortal, what is good. And what does the Lord require of you?

To act justly and to love mercy and to walk humbly with your God."

It was simple, yet profound. God wasn't asking for a perfect performance. He was asking for a surrendered heart. Trina knew this verse wasn't just advice—it was a calling. She wanted to live justly, love mercy, and walk humbly in the presence of her Creator.

Even when her life didn't look like success on paper—even when others questioned her choices—she trusted that obedience would lead her exactly where God wanted her to be.

There were days she wondered, like the rich young ruler, if living by the commandments and giving to the poor was enough. But her devotional gently reminded her: it's not the works that save us—it's the trust. Jesus paid it all. Our response is simply to believe, to receive, and to follow.

So she clung to promises like Ephesians 3:20:

"Now to Him who is able to do exceedingly and abundantly above all that we ask or imagine..."

Whenever discouragement crept in, she declared those words aloud. They weren't just hope—they were anchors.

And when fear tried to rule her mind, she chose prayer over panic. She turned her worries into worship and found peace in His presence.

There's a truth she carried deeply: we attract what we focus on. "As a man thinks in his heart, so is he." (Proverbs 23:7). By renewing her mind with Scripture, Trina learned to replace worry with wisdom, striving with surrender.

She read books like *Hung by the Tongue,* which taught her the power of her words—and more importantly, the condition of her heart behind those words. A renewed mind, a regenerated spirit, and a surrendered body—those were the ingredients of a life aligned with God.

God had shown her that affiliations—what others think of us, the titles we hold, the approval we seek—can all be eclipsed by His glory when we truly surrender.

Even when the devil tried to convince her she was too much, too late, or too broken, Trina remembered Joseph—how betrayal and prison didn't stop God's plan for his life. It *prepared* him. She realized her delays and disappointments were not detours; they were divine.

God's sovereignty didn't mean she had no part to play—it meant she had to exercise the power He gave her. He invited her to co-labor with Him through faith and obedience.

And so, she walked humbly. Loved deeply. Waited patiently.

And she praised Him, even in the in-between.

Prayer:

Father God, I come boldly before Your throne with truth in my heart. Every time a negative thought rises, help me take it captive and bring it before You. I will not be swept away by the enemy's lies. I will trust in Your promises and let the peace that surpasses all understanding guard my heart. Your Word is my anchor. I choose to live justly, to love mercy, and to walk humbly with You. In Jesus' Mighty and powerful Name and through the power of the Holy Spirit, Amen.

Compelling Argument for Time with God

The image you hold of yourself is not the one God sees.

He doesn't see you as ordinary or mediocre. He sees you through eyes of purpose and glory. You are not forgotten. You are not overlooked. You are His beloved, chosen and appointed for something extraordinary. He doesn't want you stuck in cycles of comparison or brokenness—He wants you filled with praise.

He's the one who carried you through the moments you thought would break you. And He wants to begin a deeper journey with you—one that starts not with busyness or striving, but with time. Time spent with Him. Listening. Receiving. Becoming.

We're so good at asking others, "How are you?" or turning to people when life feels off course. But what if we turned first to the One who can actually change things? What if our conversations started with heaven? What if our hearts were re-centered every morning by the One who knows every detail of our day before it begins?

You are significant—more than you know. The people who enter your life, the moments that shake you or shape you—none of it is random. It's part of God's design. And the more time you spend with Him, the clearer that becomes.

Instead of pouring out your heart to everyone else, pour it into His hands. You'll find strength. Wisdom. Direction. Hope. His visions for you are *so* big, *so* breathtaking, that He didn't want heaven without you—so He brought heaven down.

When Trina faced uncertainty, she learned to run *to* the Presence instead of away from it. She would step into her quiet space, and time after time, she'd hear gentle, powerful whispers in her spirit:

"I love you."

"You're in the right place."

"Just trust Me."

In seasons when life was pressing her with decisions and changes, those words carried her. Even when obedience meant stepping into discomfort, she could always trace the presence of peace. As she continued to meet with God, the message became consistent:

"Stay in faith."

"Be strong."

It didn't happen overnight. For a while, she simply woke up early—sometimes without clarity, sometimes without motivation—but she showed up anyway. She read her Bible. She made connections between the promises and the covenants she saw in Scripture. She began journaling. She watched as her speech changed. Complaints were replaced with praise. Regret became repentance. Fear became faith.

There was no formula—only a rhythm of faithfulness.

God was rewiring her from the inside out.

The Spirit Speaks:

"I see the burdens you've carried. The shackles that once held you—no more. In My Name, I cut them loose. Transformation begins when you give Me your wants, your needs, your desires. I have placed gifts in you, and I am awakening them. Let us commune. Let your prayers shape your worries into petitions. Give Me space to move."

Even now, that remains the most compelling argument for time with God: He moves when we make room.

Trina discovered the early hours of the day were sacred—when her heart was quietest and heaven's voice loudest. That's when perspective shifted. That's when joy returned. That's when the burdens began to feel lighter—not because life was easy, but because she wasn't carrying it alone.

Prayer:

Father God,

You know everything. I don't. Speak to me, Lord. I surrender my own wisdom, my own way, and I ask for Yours. Even when my head is barely above water, will You show me the way today? Help me to fill my mind with Your promises. Teach me to trust, even when I can't see how. I believe You are making all things right. You always do. In Jesus' Mighty and powerful Name and through the power of the Holy Spirit, Amen.

Life Is to Be One Huge Adventure After Another

There was a time when Trina didn't want to be seen, didn't want to go out, and certainly didn't want to spend money. She had just come off a high season of joy, living with her parents in Colombia—soaking in every moment of peace and simplicity. But now she was back in San Diego, where even grabbing a bite to eat felt like a luxury.

Living on $40,000 a year in one of the most expensive cities in the country wasn't easy. The average income in 2023 was nearly double that—and even that didn't stretch far. But Trina made a choice: she wouldn't open another credit card. She followed her mentor's wisdom—to live beneath her means, not just within them. And though her paycheck said one thing, her faith declared another. Some bills, she believed, were on God's tab. And time and again, He provided—in wild, unimaginable ways.

The turning point wasn't in striving harder. It was in surrender.

Trina had found a church rooted in deep community, vulnerability, and obedience. Through their Tuesday women's prayer gatherings, she discovered the power of intentional time with God. When a close friend—also Colombian—was preparing to move to Italy, Trina longed to spend time with her. But she sensed God calling her elsewhere—into the secret place, into stillness, into Him.

Each morning became sacred. She woke early to pray, worship, and journal. It wasn't a checklist—it was communion. In those quiet hours, she heard whispers like:

"I love you."

"You're in the right place."

"Just trust Me."

"Stay in faith."

"Be strong."

These weren't just affirmations. They were anchors.

At first, waking early was hard. Staying consistent was harder. But over time, that rhythm became her lifeline. Her spiritual muscles grew stronger. Her thoughts gentler. Her worries less loud. She began to trade the lies for truth.

"Keep your heart with all diligence, for out of it flow the issues of life." —*Proverbs 4:23*

She started saying out loud what she knew was true—even if her circumstances hadn't yet caught up. One of her favorite declarations came from **Jeremiah 1:12***:*

"I am watching over My Word to perform it."

And another, straight from her lips in the stillness of her room:

"God said that He will do exceedingly and abundantly more than I could ever ask or imagine!" —*Ephesians 3:20*

This intentional time with God wasn't rigid—it was life-giving. It trained her to identify and replace negative thoughts, especially during seasons when it felt like everyone else was moving forward and she was standing still.

One such moment came when engagements were popping up around her. She asked God why it wasn't happening for her, and He whispered so gently:

"You only need one man."

Peace washed over her. The striving stopped. She knew—God was writing her story, and He was faithful.

She realized that we attract what we focus on. And focusing on God—His truth, His promises, His voice—was transforming her from the inside out.

"We take captive every thought to make it obedient to Christ." —*2 Corinthians 10:5*

Her life became a living example of the scripture:

"Do not be conformed to the pattern of this world, but be transformed by the renewing of your mind." —*Romans 12:2*

God wasn't asking her to be perfect—just present.

Not powerful in her own strength—just surrendered in His.

Not always certain—just consistently faithful.

She came to believe with all her heart:

Life isn't meant to be merely endured—it's meant to be one huge adventure after another with God.

When you spend time with the Creator of your soul, the adventure unfolds, not in chaos, but in peace. You start to hear what you were created for. You start to rest in who you are. You begin to live each day expecting that God will meet you—and lead you.

So wherever you are today, start small.

Five minutes. One prayer. One moment of stillness.

"God, I'm here."

And watch—how everything begins to shift.

God Has Spoken

Trina stands firm on the promises of God. His Word—the living, breathing truth—is not far off or hard to grasp. It's available to us in many forms. As Pastor Jurgen once said, "You will reap the seeds you sow out of your mouth." Our words carry divine weight. Scripture tells us, *"Out of the abundance of the heart, the mouth speaks,"* and *"Life and death are in the power of the tongue."* These aren't just poetic truths. They are spiritual laws rooted in the unfailing Word of God.

Though Trina was raised in a home where the Bible wasn't read, her spiritual heritage ran deeper than she understood. She descended from a Spanish conquistador who fled persecution during the Inquisition, seeking religious freedom. That longing—to know God without limitation—flowed through generations, even when buried beneath cultural narratives of unworthiness. Her family once believed they were not worthy to read the Word, let alone ask anything of God.

But Trina's story became one of redemption and revelation. In a world filled with uncertainty, she often wondered, *"What's the point?"* Especially after seeing tragedies like 9/11. She once believed that living a low-key life in Hawaii, surfing and smiling, would be enough. But God had more in mind.

His plan was always rooted in love, even in grief and loss. *"Whether you eat or drink, or whatever you do, do it all for the glory of God"* (1 Corinthians 10:31). Trina came to see that even in seasons of suffering, God's hand was writing a bigger story. *"All things work together for good to those who love Him and are called according to His purpose"* (Romans 8:28). She realized she wasn't called to just "get through" life, but to walk boldly in her God-given destiny.

Her turning point came through intimacy with God. In the quiet moments of worship and surrender, she began to hear His voice: *"I love you. Stay in faith. Be strong. Just trust Me."* These weren't vague whispers—they were anchors in seasons of waiting, confusion, and hope.

Daily time with God transformed her from the inside out. Waking early to pray, journaling her faith, praising when nothing made sense—this was her lifeline. There was no formula, just a willingness to seek Him wholeheartedly. That consistency brought clarity and divine insight. It wasn't striving. It was surrender.

God began to cut off burdens and shackles in His name. He reminded her: *"Haven't I given you gifts? Don't hide. Step into your fullness. Transformation begins when you give Me your wants, needs, and desires."*

He also gave her wisdom. Like a heartbeat monitor flashing between highs and lows, she saw her spiritual rhythms. When the line dipped, she knew the answer wasn't panic—it was prayer. Prayer realigned her with heaven's perspective. *"You have not been given a spirit of fear, but of power, love, and a sound mind"* (2 Timothy 1:7). She stood tall, believing *"I am more than a conqueror through Him who loves me"* (Romans 8:37).

This truth wasn't just for her. It's for you.

Do you know who you are in Christ? Do you know that you were made to overcome?

"Who is he who overcomes the world, but he who believes that Jesus is the Son of God?" (1 John 5:5). You overcome not by trying harder but by standing in who He says you are. That's the power of faith.

Trina would declare these truths boldly—during job interviews, life decisions, and lonely nights. She didn't just recite Scripture; she embodied it.

There were seasons of solitude. No texts. No invites. Just quiet Fridays at home. But instead of seeing it as lacking, she called it peace. She learned to say, *"If something worth stepping into arises, I'll go. Until then, I'm good."* Those moments became sacred. They grounded her.

She remembered the wisdom of her mentors and refrained from financial pitfalls—even when money was tight. Trusting God's provision, she traveled to Hawaii and Puerto Rico, not out of luxury, but by faith. She had peace and joy—more valuable than anything she could buy.

Every season, every pause, every "no" became part of the greater "yes."

Because faith isn't a feeling—it's a spiritual force. *"By faith, we understand that the universe was formed at God's command"* (Hebrews 11:3). That same faith has been given to you. Faith is a frequency. Logic may explain 10% of life. But faith unlocks the remaining 90%. Faith isn't naïve—it's prophetic.

Even in moments of doubt—about career, calling, relationships—Trina returned to God. And He reminded her, *"I will do exceedingly and abundantly above all you could ask or imagine"* (Ephesians 3:20). She clung to that.

One story that mirrors this truth is that of Marcus, a man raised in poverty, discovering later in life that his parents weren't his own. He fled, brokenhearted, yet full of empathy. Through an unexpected opportunity to teach abroad, Marcus found purpose. His life shifted from survival to servanthood—helping children with birth defects, supporting veterans, and uplifting small business owners. After four battles with cancer and a heart transplant, Marcus now travels between the U.S. and Colombia, raising two beautiful daughters. His life—once marked by despair—is now a living testimony of hope, faith, and restoration.

Faith is what makes the impossible possible.

It's the key to victory. *"For whatever is born of God overcomes the world. And this is the victory that has overcome the world—our faith"*—1 John 5:4.

To live by faith is to walk in victory—no matter the circumstance. Faith doesn't bow to fear. It presses on until God's Word becomes your reality.

"I have been crucified with Christ. It is no longer I who live, but Christ who lives in me. And the life I now live… I live by the faith of the Son of God"—Galatians 2:20.

You don't need to figure it all out. Just trust the One who has spoken.

Because when God speaks… mountains move, darkness flees, and destinies unfold.

The Plowing Requires Our Authority

Many believers never fully overcome in life—not because they lack faith—but because they haven't fully understood the authority that's been entrusted to them. Trina came to realize that God designed us to create, to press forward, and to live intentionally. When she thought of "plowing," the word stirred images of cutting into hard ground—an act of courage and persistence that reaches deep into the soul.

Plowing was never meant to be passive. It's the bold motion of trust, choosing faith over fear, moving forward when God says, "Go." And with every act of obedience, His deliverance is released. Trina discovered that trusting God—even when circumstances tried to label her a victim—was the very key to reclaiming her power. Because life, if left to chance, would shape us by default. But the believer isn't called to default living. We're called to dominion.

She let go of the lie that "whatever will be, will be." That was not her anthem. That was not God's Word. From the beginning, humanity was commissioned to take dominion over the earth (Genesis 1:26). And dominion looks different for every person, in every season, but it always involves action, partnership, and divine authority.

Trina began to invite God into her decisions—not just as comfort, but as Commander. She stopped passively waiting and started actively declaring, "God, show off Your goodness. Show me what's possible." She anchored her prayers in Matthew 6:10: *"Your kingdom come. Your will be done, on earth as it is in heaven."*

Jesus has given His people the very authority of God on this earth. In Luke 10:19 (NKJV), He says, *"Behold, I give you the authority to trample on serpents and scorpions, and over all the power of the enemy, and nothing shall by any means hurt you."* That was more than a verse—it was a divine assignment.

When things felt like they were falling apart, Trina would shift her perspective. Instead of panic, she'd praise. "God," she'd pray, "nothing surprises You. You already know. I don't—but You do. I can't wait to see how You'll move in this." She learned to ask, "Give me faith. I don't even know how to believe right now. But show me. Lead me. Teach me."

She came to trust that God had hardwired desires into her spirit. Her longings weren't accidents—they were signposts pointing her back to the Creator who formed her. As she spent time with the Holy Spirit, what had once felt buried started to bloom again. Her identity awakened. Her gifts stirred. Her spiritual soil was being plowed for purpose.

The more she read Scripture, the clearer it became. In John 5:27, Jesus says, *"And He has given Him authority to execute judgment also, because He is the Son of Man."* And in verse 20, *"For the Father loves the Son and shows Him all things that He Himself does; and He will show Him greater works than these, that you may marvel."*

For Trina, the ache she sometimes felt wasn't brokenness—it was a signal. Her soul was saying: There is more. More to give. More to become. She wasn't a problem to fix; she was a vessel to be filled and a voice to be heard.

Then came a moment—quiet and unexpected—when she read a poem that shook her to her core. It stirred something holy:

"When you stop the running, and you face your soul,

It gets hard as hell—it's a winding road.

But it's in that time that you find your life.

You can run forever, or you can find your light.

Because life gets clear when we face our choices—

Were they made by us or some outside voices?

You were made for something, and only you can see it.

So stop the running—and go and be it."

It was truth wrapped in beauty. No more hiding. No more delay. The plow was in her hands. It was time to move forward with authority.

Prayer

Father God, we thank You that You've entrusted us with spiritual authority. We ask for clarity, courage, and the boldness to act when You speak. Plow the soil of our hearts and plant in us Your purpose. Strengthen our identity as sons and daughters of the Most High. Let our choices reflect heaven, and may Your power be made perfect in our obedience. In Jesus' Mighty and powerful Name and through the power of the Holy Spirit

Amen.

Grace to Your Purpose

Grace is not just a concept—it is the sustaining breath of God that carries us when everything seems like it's falling apart. It reminds us that even when life feels unmanageable, *Jesus is still King*. His love remains unchanged, even in our weakest, most broken places. Grace shows up when we think we've blown it. It covers the moments we regret, the choices we wish we could take back. It is in the grace of God that we find the strength to move forward into purpose.

Job's life is one of the most powerful portraits of this kind of grace. Amid devastating loss, he made this bold declaration:

"Though He slay me, yet will I trust Him. Even so, I will defend my own ways before Him." —Job 13:15

What kind of faith says that? A faith forged in fire. A warrior heart that refuses to give up when everything says to quit. Job teaches us that grace doesn't always look like ease—it often looks like endurance. When the weight is heavy, grace carries us to the other side.

Trina had learned this the hard way. She'd been through seasons of confusion, emotional battles, and deeply personal decisions that made her question if God could still use her. She had been attending a church that had become a spiritual home, a place where God gently peeled back the layers of her heart.

One Sunday, her favorite pastor, Pastor Becky, shared a story that pierced Trina's soul. With bold vulnerability, Pastor Becky confessed to having an abortion—and then finding out the gender of the child. The transparency of her pain mirrored something Trina had buried for years. Unspoken, untouched... until that moment.

Suddenly, shame rose like a tidal wave. Regret followed closely behind. But right there in the midst of heartache, something else arrived too: *grace*. God wasn't accusing her—He was *inviting* her. Not to stay in shame, but to let Him heal it.

Shame says, "You're not enough."

Grace says, "You are forgiven, and you are still called."

Sometimes the greatest barrier to stepping into our purpose isn't fear—it's unworthiness. But the Cross has already spoken over that. Jesus didn't wait for perfect people. He came for the wounded, the weary, and the ones who weren't sure they deserved another chance.

Trina realized her past decisions didn't disqualify her—they positioned her to testify of a Redeemer who heals. The very things she thought disqualified her became the soil in which her purpose would grow.

Let this truth settle in your soul: **He gives more grace.** —James 4:6

Not less. More. And He is not done writing your story.

Prayer

Father God, I lift every piece of my heart to You. Even the broken ones. Even the places I'm afraid to show You. Thank You that Your grace is bigger than my failures. Wash me clean. Lead me away from any path that causes regret, and into the life You've always had in mind for me. I receive Your forgiveness and walk boldly into the purpose You've placed on my life. In Jesus' Mighty and powerful Name and through the power of the Holy Spirit,

Amen.

God's Design: Surrender

Trina had been reflecting on Proverbs 18, where verse 10 reads, *"The name of the Lord is a fortified tower; the righteous run to it and are safe."* In verse 12, she noticed the wisdom: *"Before a downfall the heart is proud, but humility comes before honor."* Then came the powerful reminder in verse 21: *"The tongue has the power of life and death, and those who love it will eat its fruit."*

What tied these verses together was clear: right action begins with right thinking. And right thinking is the fruit of a heart rooted in God's Word. The more we abide in His truth, the more we begin to see as He sees, speak as He speaks, and live as He intended. There's a freedom that comes with this alignment—where the spiritual transforms the natural, and belief becomes the bridge between our circumstances and God's promises.

For Trina, that alignment didn't come easily—it came through surrender.

She had just lost her job and didn't have a stable place to live. Her finances were uncertain, but her trust in God was not. Instead of panic, she chose to move forward in prayer, trusting that God's provision would meet her where her effort and faith collided.

With intentionality, she wrote down every senior care facility she wanted to work at. She created her own system—columns for calls, checkboxes for resumes submitted, notes for follow-ups. It wasn't just job hunting; it was plowing forward in faith. She wasn't frantic—she was surrendered and prepared.

Her peace didn't come from passivity; it came from action rooted in belief. She'd ask herself each day, *"What did I do today to move closer to where God is calling me?"*

And yet, even in that strength, she knew she needed something more: the practice of surrendering her fears. Trina found that casting her anxieties on the Lord wasn't just biblical—it was vital. *"Cast all your anxiety on Him because He cares for you."* (1 Peter 5:7). It wasn't a one-time thing. It was daily. Sometimes hourly.

She learned that true surrender is the birthplace of authority. When we release control and entrust our outcomes to God, we make room for His power to move in and through us. The weights we carry—worries, regrets, disappointments—can become altars where His strength meets our weakness.

Trina began to understand something profound: "The weights of today that cause us to question our abilities and underestimate His power give Him the honor to move." When we surrender our need to control, God exceeds what we could ask or imagine. Not through striving—but through trust.

But surrender also meant forgiveness.

She learned that holding onto offense was like holding onto a spiritual weight that blocked God's best. Scripture makes it clear: *"If you forgive anyone, I also forgive him… lest Satan should take advantage of us; for we are not ignorant of his devices."*—2 Corinthians 2:10–11

Unforgiveness is the enemy's trap to keep us bound and powerless. But walking in love is our protection—it disarms his strategy. *"Be imitators of God… and walk in love."*—Ephesians 5:1–2.

Jesus made this so clear, even saying that when we stand praying, *"If you hold anything against anyone, forgive them…"*—Mark 11:25

Forgiveness unlocks faith. Letting go of offense frees our heart to fully receive.

Finding Jesus in Every Situation

Trina had come to realize something deeply profound—life doesn't slow down when things go wrong. Bills still come. People still misunderstand. Disappointment still knocks. But somewhere in the chaos, there was always a voice—soft, still, but never silent. It was the voice of Jesus, ever present, gently calling her to turn her eyes from the storm and onto Him.

Like many others, Trina faced her share of life's unpredictability. Job losses, broken relationships, health battles, family crises—it wasn't a question of *if* challenges came, but *when*. But when she truly didn't know what to do next, she discovered something invaluable: her access to God's voice.

This access wasn't reserved for the perfect or the pious. It was for the seeking heart. For the one who whispered, "Jesus, help." For the one willing to slow down and listen. Because no matter what the world tells us, we *can* hear Him. We *can* know what to do, even when we don't have it all figured out. We have something greater than the world could ever offer—a Savior who walks with us, speaks to us, and never leaves.

She remembered the words of Jesus in Luke 6:47–49:

"Everyone who comes to me and hears my words and does them... is like a man building a house who dug deep and laid the foundation on the rock. And when a flood arose, the stream broke against that house and could not shake it."

This wasn't just a story—it was a strategy. Jesus was showing us the only way to build a life that would stand through the fiercest storms. A life built not on sand, but on solid, spiritual rock.

Trina wanted her life to be well-built. She had tried temporary foundations before—relying on her own strength, leaning on others' opinions, or trying to numb her pain with distractions. But nothing held up quite like Jesus. He became her shelter, her voice of reason, and her anchor.

She began to spend her days differently. Not rushing to fix things, but retreating into God's presence. She talked to Jesus like a friend—every moment, every hour. She didn't just read Scripture; she inhaled it, letting it soak into her spirit. Her worship wasn't reserved for Sunday—it became the melody of her mornings. She surrounded herself with others who encouraged her, worshiped with her, and reminded her of who she truly was: a woman of unwavering faith.

As the storms came—and they always came—she wasn't shaken. She had found peace not in the absence of pain, but in the presence of Jesus.

Reflection Questions:

- Where in your life do you need to invite Jesus today?

- What foundation are you building your decisions on? Are you listening for His voice before moving?

A Short Prayer:

Heavenly Father, When I don't know what to do, teach me to pause and turn to You.

Help me to hear Your voice clearly and trust in Your timing completely.

Build my life upon Your truth, so when the storms come, I will not be shaken.

Thank You that I don't face life alone. You are with me in every situation

In Jesus' Mighty and powerful Name and through the power of the Holy Spirit,

Amen.

Stay in a Bubble of Love

Trina had just returned from what was supposed to be a 30-day visit with her family, which had become 40 sacred, life-giving days. Though she had made sacrifices to be there—stepping away from responsibilities and comfort—those weeks with her parents were a profound reminder of what unconditional love looked like.

Each day, her mother would gently ask, *"What are you feeling like having today?"*—then joyfully prepare whatever Trina's heart desired. The meals weren't just food; they were communion. Nourishment of the soul. Every bite reminded her she was cherished, remembered, and known. Her father, too, beamed with pride at simply having his daughter home. There was no striving there. Only presence. Only love.

But returning to San Diego brought with it an emotional and spiritual weight. She was now sleeping on a friend's bed, not paying rent—dependent on the kindness of others just to feel safe and sheltered. Despite the outward instability, Trina felt a deep longing to hear from God. She knelt down and cried out through tears, *"Jesus, please reveal what I need to hear…"*

And He did.

She heard His voice gently wash over her like waves:

"My sweet beloved Angie, please stay in faith. You are obedient to what I have called you to do. Just because you don't see anything happening does not mean there is nothing coming for you. Hold on to the prophetic words from Pastor Leanne—things are going to be **so different**.

God will do exceedingly and abundantly more than you could ever ask for or imagine! It says that in Ephesians 3:20! She said, You love to work out, but maybe that isn't where he's leading you right now. Get prepared for the next season. Claim it **in faith**, step out **in trust**.

Remember: will I not provide for you where I have called you to go? This is a great season of training for you. I will bring you what you need in **due season**.

You want to trust Me—so **practice believing**."

At that moment, Trina knew this was no longer about trying to fix everything, prove herself, or earn provision. It was about surrendering into the embrace of God's deep, steady love. He was teaching her to stay in a bubble of love—safe, still, and surrounded.

She remembered the truth from Psalm 91:1, *"He who dwells in the shelter of the Most High will rest in the shadow of the Almighty."*

Rest, not strive. Dwell, not wander.

Everywhere she looked, God had been whispering the same message:

"My daughter, stay in My love. Let My words anchor you. Let My peace hold you. Let My promises sustain you. Let My timing comfort you."

She began to recognize that love was more than a feeling. It was a **dwelling place**—a covering over her life that gave her the strength to endure and the joy to expect what was to come. When she was tempted to feel discouraged, she chose instead to believe that something was being built in the unseen.

Even when no doors seemed to open

Even when her efforts didn't seem to pay off...

Even when her prayers felt quiet...

She clung to faith. And stayed in love.

God reminded her, *"You've heard from Me. That is enough. You don't have to chase what I'm already placing in your path. You just have to walk with Me."*

She took heart in the truth from Jude 1:21, *"Keep yourselves in God's love as you wait for the mercy of our Lord Jesus Christ to bring you to eternal life."*

This was the new rhythm: Stay. Trust. Love. Repeat.

And so, Trina made the decision that would define her next season—not by circumstance, not by success, not even by clarity—but by **staying in the bubble of God's love**, where peace replaces pressure, and faith becomes sight.

Humility in the Trials

Trina knew she still had so much to learn. In every season, through every challenge, she could sense the whisper of the Lord's presence: *Calm yourself, Trina. Come to Me, and you will find Me.* That still, small voice remained her anchor.

Life was shaping her—not into someone perfect, but into someone surrendered. She had begun to realize that life wasn't about reaching some grand destination, but about becoming. Becoming the kind of woman who found Jesus in every moment.

It was a day like any other. Trina had a lively group of friends who lived moment-to-moment, planning last-minute hangouts and weekday outings. And while she loved spontaneity, she always carried a deep sense of responsibility. She was a hard worker—promoted twice in a year across different jobs, earning raises as high as $7 an hour. Yet, on this ordinary day, something extraordinary happened.

Her brother, Shawn—just returned from overseas military deployment—surprised her with a knock on the door. "Shawn?! What are you doing here?!" she cried, joy lighting up her face. Though she was moments from heading to work, everything could wait. She quickly called her boss, cancelled her meeting (a rare occurrence), and rushed out with her brother.

They ended up at a charming little coffee shop. Trina ordered her favorite toast and coffee while noticing something different about him. Shawn wasn't the same talkative young man who had left. He was quieter now, more thoughtful—like a soldier who'd seen too much too soon. A little like Channing Tatum in *Dear John*, she thought.

"So how do you feel being back?" she asked gently.

"Honestly," he said, "I'm sad. I feel like I missed out on so much. My friends are scattered... I don't even know where to find them. Everything feels unfamiliar."

Trina's heart ached. She hadn't realized how deep the wounds of absence ran. "It means the world to me that you're here," she said, holding back tears. "Canceling that meeting was easy. You're my big brother. You've always been my protector."

When he asked how *she* was doing, Trina paused. She gazed into the corner of the coffee shop, searching her heart.

"You know," she finally said, "I'm happy. I'm grateful for my life, for my job, and the people I get to work with. It's like a family. But they're not *you*. You're my real family. After Mom and Dad moved away to retire, I had to rethink everything. What kind of life do I want? I've decided to live in Charleston—and I love it. It's historic, symbolic, alive. But I want to build something real now. I want my tribe. I don't want to be alone."

Her voice softened. "I just want to attract a life filled with joy, peace, and real people. People who understand how to love, give, and forgive."

It was at that moment that Trina realized how important our mindset is. Like music, life is full of vibrations. Our thoughts play melodies that attract similar tones. The key lies in what we choose to believe.

She had learned this from scripture, especially from the powerful voices of Isaiah and Job. Job, humbled before God, once said:

"I babbled about things far beyond me, made small talk about wonders way over my head… I'm sorry—forgive me. I'll never do that again… I'll never again live on crusts of hearsay, crumbs of rumor."

There was a sacred weight in that humility. And Isaiah wrote:

"The arrogance of man will be brought low and human pride humbled; the Lord alone will be exalted on that day… People will flee to caves from the fearful presence of the Lord." (Isaiah 2:17–19)

The truth is, we don't live forever. And if we aren't living for God, then who are we really living for? Trina had finally begun to grasp that God's presence wasn't just a Sunday experience—it was a daily invitation. A divine calling to meet with the Creator, to be changed by His love, and to walk in His plan.

In quiet awe, she had learned to surrender her pride. Not just to be humbled by trials—but to *embrace* humility in them. She stopped trying to control outcomes. She let God speak. After all, as Job 42 reminds us:

"No plan of the Lord can be thwarted."

So now, Trina walks boldly, not because life is easy, but because she knows the One who guides her steps. And through that daily surrender, she's come to see the trials not as setbacks—but as holy plows that prepare the soil for miracles.

Leveling UP: Grateful Heart Momentum

Worship music had become a lifeline for Trina—a source of strength, clarity, and comfort. She had learned over time that praise was not just something you did when life felt good; it was a supernatural weapon, a declaration of trust in what could not yet be seen. It was her way of leveling up, of gaining ground in faith, no matter what life tried to throw at her.

Faith, after all, is confidence in what we hope for and assurance about what we do not see. And that faith fueled her every day, teaching her that God not only invites us to trust—He empowers us to do so.

Scripture reminded her that *"the peace that comes from the Good News prepares us for everything"* (Ephesians 6:15). And so, Trina learned to command her day. To speak healing over her life. To direct her body to worship. To cultivate gratitude as a lifestyle—not just an emotion.

Gratitude, she found, created momentum. It was the bridge between hardship and hope. It was the practice that pulled her heart away from anxiety and rooted her in truth. Habits, she realized, determine the trajectory of a life, and the habit of giving thanks—even when things didn't look right—shifted everything. She clung to Matthew 16:19:

"I will give you the keys of the kingdom of heaven. Whatever you bind on earth will be bound in heaven, and whatever you loose on earth will be loose d in heaven."

There was once a young woman Trina remembered hearing about—just 20 years old and stranded in Australia without enough money for rent or even groceries. With only faith to carry her, the woman prayed. Within hours, she received an email offering a scholarship of $500 and a phone call inviting her to work. Provision. Just like that. God's way.

These kinds of moments built Trina's trust. God would always come through. Whether she needed discipline, understanding, peace, or direction—He was the source. And when she invited Him into her day, she saw the shift.

Worship wasn't passive—it was warfare. When life felt heavy, she postured her heart with reverence and humility. Through surrender, she found strength.

Psalm 147 echoed in her spirit:

"The Lord heals the brokenhearted and binds up their wounds... He sustains the humble... He provides... He strengthens... He reveals..."

David's praise wasn't just poetic—it was powerful. It reminded her that praise brings clarity. Praise aligns our hearts with Heaven. And gratitude sets the tone for breakthrough.

Trina remembered her trip to Colombia—timed perfectly, divinely. Her grandmother had passed, and the trip allowed her to be with her parents. Time she had longed for. Time she had prayed for. Even though her finances were tight and uncertainty loomed, she stepped forward in faith. She trusted the Lord for provision, for peace, and for daily bread.

She had $200 to her name. Her passport needed renewal. Her hotel job had ended. Her car payment loomed. Her bank account dipped below zero.

Still, she praised Him for His goodness and mercy despite what was happening.

Still, she gave thanks for what she knew God could do in a moment.

Even when she missed her flight in Fort Lauderdale and had nowhere to stay, God made a way. Her mother's best friend opened her home. A few days later, her sister—without her asking—offered $200 to help. That small miracle meant everything.

It wasn't just money—it was momentum. It reminded her that God saw her. That He was working behind the scenes. That worship in the waiting made a difference.

So she gave thanks—not for the struggle, but in it.

Because gratitude releases Heaven's help.

Because gratitude keeps your heart soft when life tries to make it hard.

Because gratitude declares: "My God is faithful—even here. Even now."

A Closing Prayer:

Heavenly Father,

Thank You for being the God who sees me.

Teach me to command my day with worship and praise.

Help me build momentum with a grateful heart—one that remembers Your faithfulness in every season.

Give me eyes to see provision even in small moments.

Make me a person of praise. Let gratitude overflow from my lips and transform my life.

In Jesus' Mighty and powerful Name and through the power of the Holy Spirit,

Amen.

The Martial Arts of the Christian Life

We doubt. We fear. We lose heart. These battles show up in different ways and with varying intensity—but they come for everyone. And when they do, it can feel like you're caught in a match you weren't trained for.

But just like martial arts, the Christian life is one of discipline, strategy, and repeated practice. If you're new to the faith, start with *who* God is—not just what He can do. Talk with others who've walked with Him longer. Let their testimonies encourage you and lift your faith.

The beauty of spiritual adoption is that you now have full access to the power of God's Word. But reading it isn't enough. Like training for a match, you must *practice* declaring it. *Live it out.* Wrestle through it in the real world.

Trina once took a wrestling class, learning techniques through diagrams and demonstrations. But it wasn't until she *moved*—until she stepped onto the mat—that the process began to sink in. The Christian life works the same way. It's in the *doing* that truth takes root. It's in surrendering, relinquishing control, and trusting God even when nothing makes sense that your spiritual strength grows.

One day, Trina didn't *feel* like praying. Her heart was heavy. She was tired of the waiting. She'd been faithful—reading her Bible, journaling, worshipping—but that day, it all felt like too much. Then she walked into the kitchen of the friend's house where she was staying, and saw the words on the wall: *"Pray more. Worry less."*

She smiled. "Okay, God," she whispered. "I hear You."

Back in bed with her tea and her Bible, she asked, "What do You want me to read today?" She sensed *Esther*. She smiled and said, "I really want to read Ruth too." So she read both.

Then, it hit her.

"Blessed are you of the Lord, my daughter," she read in Ruth 3:10. "You have shown more kindness at the end than at the beginning... do not fear. I will do for you all that you request, for all the people of my town know that you are a virtuous woman."

Trina wept.

This was God. He was reminding her that He *sees* her. That even when she feels like nothing is happening—something *is*. He's training her. Preparing her. Watching over her.

Just the night before, she'd been watching a video on Christian dating in her car, pondering how much she still had to learn. Ironically, right then a young man she'd recently met appeared. She chuckled to herself at the divine timing. As she watched him interact with his dogs and neighbors, she thought, *Maybe life really is a series of learning experiences. Maybe it's okay to not have it all figured out.* She was beginning to believe that God had been speaking all along. She just had to tune in.

Later, in the book of Esther, the words leapt off the page again: *"...for such a time as this."* (Esther 4:14). She'd read it before, but this time it landed differently. *What if* all this—every detour, every closed door—was part of the design?

Reading further, she saw how Queen Vashti's defiance opened the door for Esther to step into a greater purpose. Esther didn't need to be perfect. She just needed to be *available.* And so does Trina. And so do you.

God doesn't need your performance—He wants your participation. He wants your surrender.

And when you show up in obedience, His favor does the rest.

"But without faith, it is impossible to please Him, for he who comes to God must believe that He is, and that He is a rewarder of those who diligently seek Him." — Hebrews 11:6

A Prayer for Strength and Surrender

Father God, You orchestrate every detail of our lives. You know where we've come from and what we need for where we're going. Thank You for this season of preparation. Thank You for reminding us that it's not about striving, but surrendering. Even when we feel inadequate or unsure, You see us. You reward our seeking. Thank You for giving us grace in the wrestling and power in the Word. Teach us to train well in the faith, to grow strong in perseverance, and to wait with hope. We trust You. We honor You. In Jesus' Mighty and powerful Name and through the power of the Holy Spirit name,

Amen.

The Design of Our Lives: Who's Your Neighbor?

When Trina first arrived in San Diego ten years ago, she didn't come armed with unshakable faith—she came with a gift someone had once prayed over her: the seed of trust. At the time, she lacked confidence in God's plan and struggled to rely on anything outside her own strength. But over time, through situations that didn't go as planned—disappointments in work, heartache in relationships—she began to lean not on her own understanding, but on something greater.

The change didn't come overnight. It came through community.

Trina found herself surrounded by believers whose stories couldn't be denied. Their testimonies were contagious. She saw miracles unfold—some in her life, others in theirs—and her heart began to soften. She began to pray, not just with obligation but with a genuine desire to know God. Asking Him for what she needed taught her something that self-reliance never could: vulnerability is not weakness. It's the doorway to growth.

Her friend Justin once shared how surrendering his desires as a man was a spiritual journey. Trusting God in his battle against temptation wasn't just about willpower—it was about wisdom. He leaned on godly counsel and trusted that God's design was better than his own impulses. For Justin, the journey to freedom wasn't isolation; it was community. It was being known. "Sometimes," he said, "you just need to know someone truly cares." And don't we all?

People want to ask you questions. They want to be part of your life. If no one modeled love and care for you in the way you needed, God can still send people who will. That's why prayer is so powerful. It prepares our hearts to *receive* love and community. Because the real question isn't just "Who is your neighbor?"—it's "Are you willing to let them in?"

Another friend, Kim, opened up about her fear of becoming like her father. She didn't want to replicate his attitude or bitterness. Recognizing that fear was the first red flag—and it led her to a deeper place of honesty with herself and with God. Vulnerability, she realized, was the beginning of healing. It exposed old wounds that were still speaking.

Trina, too, had her moment of reckoning. For so long, she never asked God for help. Deep down, she thought asking made her weak. She was raised to be strong, self-sufficient—to *figure it out*. But eventually, she saw the lie in that belief. It was time to cancel the narrative running through her mind that she had to carry it all alone. It had metastasized in her thinking for too long.

Then came the breaking point.

Everything around her looked bleak. Her resources were gone. Her strength was low. Her hope was flickering. She stood at the crossroads of despair and belief—and in that moment, she chose to trust. Not because she had a guarantee, but because she had a *God*.

She dared to ask, *"Could He really help me in the middle of this?"*

"Could God actually move in ways that defy the natural?"

Sometimes, the greatest gift God gives us is an opportunity to deepen our relationship with Him—not by giving us answers, but by drawing us into deeper trust. The question isn't whether we have all the answers—it's whether we'll have even 1% of faith that He does.

When we mix the spiritual with our day-to-day lives, we begin to see how every situation is designed not just to stretch us, but to *transform* us. Even hard things can expose the very areas where our faith is growing. And often, that transformation happens in community. Friends become mirrors. They reflect our blind spots. They lift our burdens. They remind us of what's possible when we forget.

When you can't see from God's perspective, look through the eyes of those He's placed around you.

A Prayer of Trust and Clarity

Father God, I come before You humbly, knowing that only You truly understand where I've come from and what has shaped me. You know the silent struggles, the quiet doubts, the questions I've been too afraid to ask. Today, I surrender them all. I invite You to take full control of my life—my thoughts, my patterns, and my perspective. Speak to me, Lord. Show me what needs to change. Make me aware of anything holding me back. Help me step fully into the life You've designed for me. Lead me in Your truth. In Jesus' Mighty and powerful Name and through the power of the Holy Spiritname,

Amen.

Talking to One Another

There came a time in Trina's life when she found herself confronted by a new kind of truth—one that arrived not through sermons or Scripture, but through the people who lived just a few feet away.

Her apartment in San Diego was cozy and filled with warmth, the kind of place that hosted weekly dinners and friendly laughter. But it was also where life, in all its messiness, pressed in from every direction. Her neighbor, Stacey, was outspoken and often unpredictable, while her own roommate stayed up late most nights drinking and painting. The noise, the tension, the spiritual unrest—it began to weigh on Trina's soul.

One afternoon, while walking to her car, Stacey remarked sharply, "You make a lot of noise, you know."

It stung, but more than that, it stirred something. The Lord began whispering, "Be a neighbor."

Convicted, Trina realized she hadn't truly asked what Stacey needed or why there was such tension. After her roommate offhandedly revealed a past entanglement with Stacey, it all began to make sense. Wounded people often wound others—and Trina knew she was called to something different.

So she invited Stacey to dinner. To community. To conversation. And surprisingly, Stacey came. The late-night visitors stopped. Her walls came down.

Then, a few days later, Trina received an enormous bouquet—48 red roses. No note. No name.

Eventually, Stacey admitted it had been her. "Thank you for being a good neighbor," she said through tears. "Can we talk sometime?"

And they did. They walked together. Shared their hearts. Prayed.

Stacey opened up about her brokenness, her desire to stop prostituting herself, and her longing for something pure and lasting. She moved to Sacramento, found healing, and eventually placed her faith in Jesus. Miraculously, her symptoms of bipolar disorder lifted as she began walking in the truth of who God said she was.

But it wasn't just Stacey who experienced healing. Trina did, too.

Through that open door of friendship and obedience, God began to expose hidden places in Trina's heart. She realized she had carried a deep, unspoken belief that she wasn't worthy of love—not from people, and certainly not from God.

It wasn't until she formed a new friendship with a woman at church named Tammy that she had the courage to voice it.

"I don't feel like I deserve love," Trina confessed one day. "Not after everything that's happened. I want healing. I want forgiveness. But I don't know how to receive it."

Tammy gently listened and then prayed with her. They asked God to reveal the root of that lie, and in that moment, the Lord took Trina back to her twenties—to a trauma she had buried for years. A moment when she had been sexually abused and told herself it was somehow her fault. That she had forfeited the right to feel pure. To feel loved.

But God, in His mercy, met her there.

Tears fell freely as Trina released the pain, the shame, and the anger. She gave it all to Jesus—finally. And in return, He gave her peace. He reminded her of who she was: beloved, redeemed, whole.

Healing began that day. Not all at once, but in layers. Through every prayer. Every conversation. Every time she chose to believe His voice over her past.

Prayer

Heavenly Father, You are the God who sees—nothing is hidden from You. You know the moments that broke us, and the lies we believed because of them. I lift up every place in me that still aches, still wonders if I am truly loved. I ask You to uncover the roots of shame, pain, and unworthiness, and to uproot them with Your mercy. Help me to receive Your healing like rain over dry ground. Help me to trust You with the parts of my story I've buried deep. Thank You for placing people in my life who point me back to You. May every conversation be a door that leads me closer to Your heart.

In Jesus' Mighty and powerful Name and through the power of the Holy Spirit, Amen.

Prayer

Father God, Help me to find You in every situation. Thank You for the way You orchestrate our lives—intertwining our paths with those who need Your love. May I carry Your heart to those around me. Teach me to be bold, kind, and obedient to Your Spirit. Let every conversation, even the awkward ones, become invitations for healing and transformation.

In Jesus' Mighty and powerful Name by the power of the Holy Spirit,

Amen.

Exciting Journey Awaits

Trina had once believed that the only way to be taken care of was through her own diligence and hard work. She was raised in a world where striving was necessary and provision felt conditional. But even with all of her drive and relentless effort, she still found herself overwhelmed by a hidden anxiety—a fear of not having enough. Not enough money. Not enough love. Not enough strength.

Months went by where Trina carried the silent burden of worry. She didn't speak of it often, but it weighed heavily on her. She would stay up late, her thoughts spinning with questions about how she would afford the next bill, how she would handle the unexpected, how she could possibly sustain the pace of the life she was living.

But somewhere in the quiet, she started to hear something different. A whisper in her spirit began to break through the noise. "Fearing people is a dangerous trap, but trusting the Lord means safety." That verse from Proverbs 29 softened her heart. It drew her into a place of surrender. Her eyes began to lift— not to her bank account, her work calendar, or her plans—but to God.

It was in this space of surrender that Trina came to know the truth of Jeremiah 29:11—not just as a verse quoted in passing, but as a living promise. "'For I know the plans I have for you,' declares the Lord, 'plans to prosper you and not to harm you, plans to give you a hope and a future.'" And that hope began to take root in her heart.

She started to walk differently. Talk differently. She was no longer moved by fear, but by trust. Trust in a God who never failed her. Who provided in the most unexpected of ways. When she was down to her last few dollars, help came. When she felt isolated and unseen, someone reached out. When her strength gave way, His peace stepped in.

Over time, that trust turned into joy. Joy rooted in a God who said, "I will supply all your needs according to My riches in glory through Christ Jesus." Her life became a testimony to God's faithfulness—not because everything was easy, but because He was always enough.

And the key that unlocked this trust? Obedience.

She didn't always understand what God was asking her to do. Sometimes it didn't make sense. But she followed anyway. Because she began to believe that doing it simply because God said so was enough. That obedience wasn't about understanding—it was about trust. And trust was the soil where peace could finally grow.

Today, Trina lives differently. Where generations before her carried the chains of worry and fear, she walks freely. She wakes up without dread. She faces unknowns with confidence. Not because she knows what's coming, but because she knows Who is leading her.

Her journey is still unfolding, but one thing is certain: she's no longer journeying alone.

A Prayer of Trust

Father God, Thank You for the promise that Your plans for us are good. You are the God of provision, the One who leads and never forsakes. I surrender my need to understand and control. Teach me to trust You deeply—beyond what I see, beyond what I feel. Help me obey, simply because You said to. Let my life reflect Your faithfulness. Free me from fear and fill me with Your peace. As it says in Psalm 121:1-2, " I lift up my eyes to the mountains-where does my help come from? My help comes from the Lord, the maker of the Heaven and Earth. We praise you for what you are doing in the background. We trust you, Father God. In Jesus' Mighty and powerful Name and through the power of the Holy Spirit,

Amen.

Don't Waste the Seasons

Every season holds a key. And within that key is an invitation—not only to unlock a new outcome, but to unlock a new version of yourself in God's power. Trina had come to know this in the most unexpected of ways. She had learned to not limit God. He could do far more than she ever could think or imagine.

One autumn, she went with friends to an Escape Room downtown. At first, it was just a fun Friday night plan, something lighthearted after a long week. But by the time the night ended, she found herself reflecting deeper than expected.

Each room had its own puzzle. Each puzzle, a code or clue. To move forward, they needed to unlock three things. Later that evening, sitting around a table with laughter and leftovers, Trina couldn't shake the feeling—this was a picture of her spiritual walk.

The first room taught her something simple but radical: *Don't be afraid of your dreams.* The clue had said, "Dare to dream." And in her heart, she felt the Spirit speak, *It's the right choices that lead to the abundant life I have for you.* Believing that truth changed everything. Because when you dare to dream with God, you move into partnership with the One who designed your destiny.

The second room's clue was just as powerful: "You are the salt of the earth." It hit her with clarity—she needed to preserve her purpose, stay in peace, and continue moving forward even when things felt uncertain. Salt wasn't just seasoning; it was sacred. Losing her "saltiness" meant losing her impact. Her value.

In the third room, there was a riddle about regret and worry. She was instructed to "dump or not to dump" each marble. Trina saw herself standing over a scale, holding stones from her past—disappointments, trauma, betrayals. What if, instead of trying to measure their weight herself, she gave them to God? What if *He* was her scale? She remembered Psalm 55:22, *"Cast your burdens on the Lord and He will sustain you."* She knew God had been wanting her to release her difficulties and worries. Her anxieties needed to go into the hands of a God who cares for her more than she understood.

Then came the fourth room. "Write the vision," it read. It was in letters jumbled up that had to spell a 4 letter word, "Join". She recalled in Habakkuk 2:2

"And The Lord said to me, Write The vision, and make it plain upon tables..." Habukuk 2:3 says, "For the vision is yet for an appointed time, but at the end it shall speak, and not lie: though it tarry, wait for it; because it will surely come, it will not tarry." Trina remembered the dreams she had buried, the callings she had doubted, and she began to write. And when she wrote, healing flowed.

In the final room, the words glowed in gold letters at the exit: "Wait, and Trust". She thought, "Wait on the Lord. Continue to walk in trust" as it says, "Psalm 27:14: "Wait for the Lord; be strong and take heart and wait for the Lord."

The timing wasn't hers to control. The outcome wasn't hers to force. But the promise was hers to hold.

What she realized that night—and in the seasons since—was this: Trust always generates a power from the Living God to move. Especially when we share it thoughtfully and prayerfully. Every testimony carries within it the spark to ignite someone else's freedom. When she spoke of the battles she had faced, it was never just about her survival—it was about pointing others to their own breakthrough.

Seasons, she discovered, are not wasted when they're surrendered. Even the hard ones. Especially the hard ones.

Trina began to see how God used even her workplace to reveal these truths. For years, she had given so much of herself to be the best, to perform, to earn her keep. But she came to see that her identity was never in her title. Never in her paycheck. Never in being the most reliable. Her value and worth came from the One who formed her in His image (Genesis 1:27), who called her a *handiwork* (some versions of the Bible say masterpiece) and designed her with a divine purpose prepared in advance —Ephesians 2:10.

Even though she wanted a good job and to be reliable (previously mentioned to be an important value in society) it felt like she had been chasing the idea that *actions* instead of *resting* were leading her into the purpose of *being* who she was *made* to be at that time.

Now, with every new season, she viewed her life more clearly: It's not about perfection. It's about purpose. It's not about hustling for approval—it's about walking in obedience doing the best she could. Obedience was the key that unlocked her trust. Trusting in this season she lived always led to peace and joy if she knew her identity as a beloved Daughter or King of Christ Jesus..

A Heartfelt Prayer

Heavenly Father, Thank You for the design of every season. For the clues You leave behind in moments we don't always understand. I pray that we would not waste the trials, the waiting, the victories—or even the pain. Instead, help us to see that *You are in all of it.* Christ Jesus, I ask for a humble revelation of your love for your beloved and a greater dependency on You. Let us not be trapped by fear of others nor of this world to lead us astray. I declare we learn to walk freely in trusting You humbly. We know it says, *"Fearing people is a dangerous trap, but trusting the Lord means safety"* —*Proverbs 29:25.*

Thank you for letting us into obedience to become our act of worship and our heart filled with trust to be the song that carries us forward. Fill us with the assurance that You will provide for all our needs according to Christ's riches in glory.

Teach us to live like you want us to live, guarding our steps. Sharing about you and resting in the truth that Your power is released every time we choose to walk in faith and speak in love.

We love You. We trust You. We surrender this season to You.

In Jesus' mighty name and by the power of the Holy Spirit,

Amen.

Serving is the Answer: The Becoming

We are called to love and serve one another. That call rests within the boundaries of God's beautiful design for our lives. For Trina, leaving behind a secular vocation wasn't part of the original vision—but God had a deeper transformation in store. As she grew in her walk with Christ, she began to live out the truth in **1 Corinthians 7:17–24**:

"Only let each person lead the life that the Lord has assigned to him, and to which God has called him… So, brothers, in whatever condition each was called, there let him remain with God."

These verses became an anchor for Trina. They reminded her that God's providence and sovereignty are not confined to ministry roles or religious settings. Even in marriage, it says in 1 Corinthians 7 33, "But a married man has to think of his earthly responsibilities and how to please His wife. His interests are divided, In the same way, a woman who is no longer married or has never been married can be devoted to the Lord and hold in body and in spirit. But, a married woman has to think about her earthly responsibilites and how to please her husband." It goes on to sharehow the Lord wants you to have few distractions as possible.

Whether working in hospitality, education, or business, God assigns us each a territory where we can reflect His glory. She came to see her workplace not as a limitation, but as an invitation—to trust God in the position He had placed her and to make much of Him there.

Jesus Himself transitioned from carpentry to full-time ministry at thirty (Luke 3:23), modeling how divine timing aligns with divine calling. Paul reminded the early believers that after conversion, our role is to trust God's placement, even when emotions tell us otherwise. As Trina embraced this, she stopped striving to escape her job and began asking, *"God, how can I reveal who You are right where I am?"*

When seeking direction, she reflected on these questions: *What brings me joy? What stirs my passion? What do I do well?* These became her compass, always pointing back to the truth that every vocation—no matter how ordinary—is an opportunity to glorify God. As **1 Timothy 1:6** says, *"Fan into flame the gift of God which is in you."*

And here's where it all started to unfold:

"If you lift the limitations you've placed on yourself and open your heart to even the smallest spark of interest, God can lead you into the perfect assignment—one designed to reveal the clues hidden in each room and riddle of your life's journey."

Trina began to see her career not merely as work, but as worship. Her heart softened toward her coworkers, even in the midst of difficult situations. The words of Christ echoed in her spirit: *"Forgive them, for they do not know what they are doing,"* and *"Greater love has no one than this: to lay down one's life for one's friends."* She began to understand that serving meant laying down pride, comfort, and even the need for recognition—choosing instead to love well, reflect grace, and show up with humility. This was the *becoming*: learning that the workplace could become holy ground when surrendered to God.

God had not abandoned her to the world; He had sent her into it. Her faith became alive in the "ordinary" as she bore witness to God's fingerprints everywhere. Even when jobs shifted, she remained planted in love. And in doing so, she learned that every role, every task, and every conversation could become sacred offering.

God's will is at work in every age, through every act of love, service, and surrender. Trina's purpose was no longer attached to titles, income, or applause—it was rooted in obedience to the One who called her. She came to see, through Romans 8:28, that *"in all things God works for the good of those who love Him, who have been called according to His purpose."*

She had been called—from every vocation, for every season—to serve well, love deeply, and live fully within the territory assigned by God. Trina began to understand that every chapter of her life was sacred, no matter the setting. Her training as a first responder for homeless veterans became more than a job; it was preparation for kingdom work.

One St. Patrick's Day in Pacific Beach, San Diego, she felt an undeniable nudge from the Holy Spirit. The streets were buzzing with festivity, but her heart was drawn elsewhere. Led down an alley beside the boardwalk, she came upon a man slouched against a wall, visibly drunk. Compassion stirred within her. "Hey, are you okay?" she asked gently. "I'm fine... just really struggling, but I'm good," he replied. She could hear the pain in his voice. She looked him in the eye and said with quiet boldness, "Jesus loves you so much. I believe He sent me here just for you."

Moved by God's love, she invited him to church. To her amazement, he met her the next day, just as they had planned. Not only did he attend church with her, but he also connected with Pastor Mark from Awaken Church, who helped him take a brave next step—entering an inpatient program to receive treatment for alcohol dependency. His name was Christian.

Two months later, Christian called Trina. His voice was full of life. He told her she had saved him. But Trina knew—it wasn't her. It was God, working through obedience. She could take no credit. She had simply followed His prompting. What once seemed like just another day had become a divine appointment. After seven years of drinking a handle of vodka every day, Christian had found freedom. And Trina knew deep in her soul: *this* is what it meant to be used by God—for such a time as this.

Pour out your heart to Him if you need guidance. Just know that He is wanting us to be faithful with our living in love to others with God's commandments. Keep joyfully magnifying Christ—people need to see that whatever you do, God will get the glory, and if you pour out your heart more, you can take the cross to enjoy the way we worship Him to carry out His desires when we speak it forth in our everyday life. If we do the work by asking Him in prayer it's enough! Keep in mind a few things, "Forgive them for they do not know what they are doing" if they treat you wrong. Moreover, "Hath no greater love than a man who lays down their life for someone else" if you are called to help those who help others.

Working in the "world" isn't necessary when we see how God's will in this age is always done. You will see Him if you choose to ask him for help. Then you can say, "Wow, that was Him for sure!" And then learn to share how Anything is possible for God in the best way you can. He calls us into a needy world where all the suffering will reveal his glory as it says in Romans 8:28. Trina realized that Loving those in the world was her job. Staying at peace with her identity in Jesus as it comes to living as Royalty. Men and Women of God are treated as the ones who see unexpected favor in the 1% out of 99%. That's what she started to see in her life! We are called to live Limitless as we love our neighbors as ourselves. "That my friends has served God's kingdom well."

Suggestion for meditating and worshipping Our Creator who has designed a special plan for you, "Worshipping Your Plan Is" by Josie Buchanan.

Father God, Thank You for the gift of worship. Thank You that praise is not just music, but a weapon, a lifeline, and a gateway to Your presence. Teach me to choose gratitude when it's hard, to lift my voice when I feel low, and to trust that You are always working behind the scenes. May my heart overflow with thankfulness, and may my life reflect the beauty of trusting You in every season.

In Jesus' mighty and powerful Name and through the power of the Holy Spirit,

Amen.

Are you Ready to Live Out Your Purpose?

How Satan prevents True Restoration. If you are smoking, damaging your lungs the enemy is silencing your voice that was meant to praise Him.

If you have crippling self-doubt or insecurity, you are more likely to lead or inspire.

If you are dangerous to the darkness, the enemy is muting your confidence.

If you are experiencing distractions and procrastination you carry vision, strategies, and ideas. More importantly, the enemy cannot stop you therefore he uses you to stop yourself.

If you struggle with lust and pornography, you have a deep capacity for intimacy and healing.

If you struggle with perverting love that prevents true restoration.

Fear of rejection or abandonment means you carry a spirit of belonging and reconciliation. You were meant to gather the outcasts and not to make you feel like an outcast.

If you struggle with body appearance, that's because you were meant to reflect God's glory not the world's standards. When you're drawn to witchcraft, astrology, God has a special plan for you. You have a prophetic gift. The enemy counterfeits it to keep you out of alignment. Only he knows what's for you and how to bring it to you.

Chances are you are ready to live out your purpose. Here are some **tips for articulating your biblical purpose:**

1. Keep it short.

2. Focus more on "being" than on "doing." (Your purpose clarifies who God has shaped you to be. Understanding who God made you to be will prepare you to discover and pursue God's vision for your life.)

3. Use language that grips and energizes you. Pray, "Father in Heaven, You are Holy and Beloved. Thank you for shaping my life the way it

is. I believe you have a purpose in everything you do. I pray for help to guide me to my purpose. Release Help for me to have my purpose revealed. Light the path, show me the way. I know that it is because of the Words from the Bible that they go out to accomplish what they have been set out to do. You are the best. And I trust you. In Jesus' mighty name and through the power of the Holy Spirit.Examples of biblical purpose statements

- "I live to bring glory to my Lord and Savior Jesus Christ through consistent worship, by my praise and in my life; to cultivate a life of intimacy with God; and to equip women and men for ministry through the power of the Holy Spirit."

- "The purpose of my life is to know God and hear his voice so I can live a life of servanthood and obedience; then, I will be a God-defined person and a non-anxious presence in every situation.

- "I exist to live in authentic intimacy with Jesus and let him shape my life in such a way that believers are encouraged and unbelievers are motivated to join me in the journey of discipleship. This is the story of a girl who lived in a way that was unexplainable. What everyone would have called luck started on a very sunny day. It was June time. Trina used to walk around saying hi to every individual or at least trying to catch their eye. She had been living in San Diego. The luck people thought was ensuing in her life was because she lived in a beautiful place. Expensive too. Money was honestly never a big issue. Even while she was living a very limited life financially. Still to this day buying clothes and going on was not constant by any means. She walked around, cautious of where to spend her time and money, but the lack thereof was never important. Gradually, things have gotten better. There was a period of time where going out to eat in nice places was a random occurrence. She knew that she was never to worry and live in abundance. She came to San Diego 9 years ago to be able to live by the beach. She knew one could live a stress free life by doing so. Living close to it and walking near the coast every day. What a life! There was the mentality given by Trina's parents, it doesn't matter where you live as long as you have the ability to sustain yourself financially. Having "responsibility" was the main focus in learning how to live.

You are Stronger Than You Think

A huge reminder of the power we hold is summed up in the exact amount of adversity we have been through. It's not indicative of what we can handle at any given time. When it happens, you can choose to have strength and belief in the things that you have overcome. When you are digging deep. I am sure not everyone can withstand huge amounts of challenges for a prolonged period of time. What I do know is we can choose to believe that we will withstand any situation. Joel Osteen in Your Best Life now says, "As a rule of thumb, the more positive your thoughts and words, the stronger you will be and the sooner you will get over whatever ails you." God has promised to develop your character by taking you to a higher level with more character and discipline.

This is where we hold our power. Channeling our strength comes from that which is within. Mastering yourself to the point of encouraging yourself to take it a bit further. Opening yourself to have someone share a prophecy that holds the calling to our destiny will give us the key to unlock this power of belief through courage. I would not want you to exhibit unappreciation for the Bible, commonly referred to as truth. I trust that one day, you will experience Abraham's blessings. Abraham's blessings are for us. Not just for his descendents! The blessing of Abraham might come on the Gentiles through Jesus Christ. The chapter was in Galatians 3:14, 29, "That the blessing of Abraham might come on the Gentiles through Jesus Christ...And if ye be Christ's, then are ye Abraham's seed, and heirs according to the promise."

Abraham's blessing is yours! Through Jesus Christ! We are going to keep finding ourselves in full supply. God did not promise we would have a lean supply but a "rich" supply. We are abundantly provided for! Praise God forevermore! God has redeemed us from the curse of poverty! God has promised to make each one of us rich! He wants to show you His love, His faithfulness, and His goodness!

"Life is about knowing that you will walk through the doors you once prayed would open."

Speaking it out, life-giving sentences, "I am valuable, I am loved. God has a great plan for my life. Everything I touch prospers and succeeds. I'm excited about my future."

Dialogue: *Search your Heart*

Do you have faith that moves mountains? If not, I want to speak to you about addressing this idea. I believe that where your attention goes, energy flows.

Are you patient to inherit the kingdom? Why is it easy to get frustrated? Do you trust God has the best itinerary for your life?

Your perspective is the one thing that must change. It's gotta be brought to an awareness. A level playing field where any person can attest that you have "that" understanding. Whether you are growing is all good. It all serves a purpose.

The Plan for Your Life

For Trina, life in San Diego wasn't always easy. On the days when she didn't "feel" like showing up, she had to remind herself of something deeper than emotion: her calling. Over time, she learned to see the significance of simply being faithful—of showing up and sowing into relationships even when life felt quiet or unclear. Looking back, she realized much of her growth had come not through grand moments, but through simple, steady obedience.

Trina learned to serve the purpose in front of her with all her heart. She began to understand that the plan for her life wasn't just a future destination—it was a daily process of growing: growing in love, in compassion, in generosity, and in taking responsibility for her life. Even if she made mistakes and was far from perfect. She continued to ask for wisdom and guidance. She was created, as we all are, to glorify God—not just in church, but in every sphere of life. As scripture says, *"Bring my sons from afar and my daughters from the end of the earth—everyone who is called by my name, whom I created for my glory."*

And yet, there was something foundational that Trina had to master: forgiveness. Forgiveness became her key, unlocking peace in her life and freedom in her heart. She came to understand that following Christ meant extending mercy to everyone—even when they didn't deserve it. After all, Jesus said, *"By this, all people will know that you are my disciples, if you have love for one another"* (John 13:35). And love, she learned, keeps no record of wrongs.

Every morning, Trina would quiet her heart in prayer, asking God to help her see others as He sees them.

Dear God, open my mind to the things I do not understand. Guide me to be more patient and compassionate to the people around me. Touch my heart and allow me to see the good in all things. I humbly ask You to help me forgive those who've wronged me. In Jesus Mighty and powerful Name and through the power of the Holy Spirit Amen.

Her days often started normally. But even in the quiet, Trina felt a deep desire for more. She could sense there was more to this life than routines and survival. She believed life was a never-ending journey of becoming the best version of herself—whether she chose to lean into that or not. And as she spoke with friends who encouraged her spirit, it felt like puzzle pieces locking into place: the waiting, the quiet, the daily showing up. It was all part of the process.

She realized something powerful: Life wasn't happening to her. It was happening for her.

Her mindset shifted. Each day became an opportunity to fight—not for survival, but for purpose. Whether she was pursuing her goals, nurturing friendships, or chasing dreams, Trina understood now that life was like a symphony. Every choice created a note. And with the right choices, she could build a life that sang.

Ultimately, she understood her life was about trust—learning to trust a God who had a plan, even when she couldn't see it. A God who called her to forgive, to love, to grow, and to trust that His ways were better than her own.

Because the truth is: that kind of life—the one full of grace, purpose, and trust—does exist.

And Trina was learning to live it.

Embracing the Obstacles

Obstacles once felt like barriers to Trina. But over time, she began to wonder—could they actually be invitations? Invitations to love herself enough to overcome. To believe that what she faced wasn't punishment, but preparation. Maybe God's plans included the struggle because He loved her too much to leave her unshaped.

Trina remembered the season when she left everything behind to take time for herself. She had envisioned rest, healing, maybe even peace. But when the time came, she battled. The quiet was uncomfortable. Rest felt like work. Slowing down meant facing the thoughts she'd long avoided. Though she enjoyed sweet moments of peace, learning to live in the overflow of God's presence didn't come easily.

She thought of Zacchaeus, the tax collector who climbed the sycamore tree just to catch a glimpse of Jesus. And yet, it wasn't until Jesus called him down that transformation began. Zacchaeus had to *come down* from his striving, his hiding, and meet Jesus face to face. Trina realized she needed to do the same.

One night, exhausted by the internal struggle, Trina prayed a simple but vulnerable prayer:

"Lord, show me how much You love me."

And He answered.

For nearly two months, Trina felt wave after wave of affection like she had never known. She wept often—not from sadness, but from feeling whole. His love didn't just comfort her; it changed her. The affection of God became her healing. She understood now: it wasn't discipline that drew her into right living, it was love.

God's love will always cause you to come closer, not by force, but by desire.

But just as she found breakthrough, new obstacles appeared. Doubt. Fatigue. Fear. In those moments, Trina remembered the Israelites wandering in the wilderness. In *Battlefield of the Mind*, Joyce Meyer wrote about the "wilderness mentality"—how the children of Israel wandered forty years, not because God withheld, but because they couldn't let go of the mindset that kept them bound.

Trina knew their story was a warning.

She could wander too, if she chose to rehearse her fears. She could stay on the same mountain, cycling through old patterns. But God was calling her forward.

"You've dwelt long enough at this mountain," she felt the Lord say. *"It's time to move on."*

The choice was hers.

And so, she set her mind on what was above. She chose gratitude even when the evidence felt scarce. She replaced negative thoughts with declarations of trust. With whispered prayers in the quiet, she told God she believed Him— even when she didn't feel it yet.

She learned to speak to her life. To command fear to flee. To declare over her own future. Worship became her weapon, music her ally. Praising before she saw the victory.

She remembered the words from 2 Timothy 2:10:

"So I am willing to endure anything if it will bring salvation and eternal glory in Christ Jesus to those God has chosen."

Maybe, just maybe, every obstacle she faced wasn't just about her. Maybe it was about those she was called to reach.

Victory, she realized, wasn't just a feeling. It was a spiritual reality that generated power from the living God the moment she chose to believe.

And so, she pressed on.

God's Provision: The Leverage

Trina finally stopped trying to earn God's love. Instead of striving, she began to receive.

She'd heard the verse countless times— *"We love because He first loved us"* (1 John 4:19)—but now, it was real. She knew in her heart: there was nothing she could do to make God love her more or less. His love was steady, constant, and unconditional. It was this love—not duty or fear—that changed her heart. Slowly, shame melted. Guilt lifted. Fear lost its grip.

When she boarded the flight to San Diego, she carried more than her suitcase. She carried hope that this new chapter would be different. Her father had left a book about San Diego on their family coffee table when she was young, and now, she believed it was more than coincidence.

A company had invited her for an interview after weeks of uncertainty. And even though it wasn't guaranteed, Trina sensed God was asking her to trust.

Soon, she was staying with a family friend, helping care for a seven-month-old baby in the mornings. It wasn't glamorous—but it was a start. From there, doors opened: a role in a retirement home, where her years as a speech therapist could once again serve others.

One night, while working as an overnight caregiver for a woman with dementia, she felt at peace. She was exactly where God wanted her. Yet life shifted quickly. After a simple misunderstanding over a bottle of wine left near the woman's medication, Trina found herself being asked to leave.

It felt like a door slamming shut.

With nowhere to go, she called Valerie—the family friend who'd invited her to San Diego in the first place. Valerie picked her up and drove her to the cliffs overlooking La Jolla Shores. But instead of offering comfort, Valerie handed her a plane ticket home. Trina sat in stunned silence. Her faith felt small. Surely, God hadn't brought her this far just to send her back.

And then she remembered Kathleen. A woman she'd met at a nursing conference weeks prior.

One call changed everything.

Kathleen answered—and offered Trina a place to stay in Del Mar. A home of peace, surrounded by beauty. Over the holidays, Trina found herself reflecting: just when she thought her journey was over, God had provided again.

From there, more doors opened. A job at an award-winning memory care facility. New friendships. A community that felt different from anything she'd known in Washington, D.C. People in California were open. Honest. Free.

She met a man, too—an Italian with a kind smile who introduced her to his circle of Christian friends. They weren't perfect, but their love felt pure, unpretentious. They loved for love's sake.

And then, the ocean. The cliffs. The flowers. Daily walks became her therapy. Even when working forty hours a week, she'd find herself at the beach—breathing in freedom. Healing. Slowly, she realized that God wasn't just meeting her needs. He was writing a love story with her life.

One day, as she stood by the water, she heard a quiet whisper in her spirit:

"This is your leverage. Faith is your leverage. My provision, not your striving, is the path forward."

She remembered a sermon where a pastor compared walking with Jesus to stepping out of a boat. Jesus was already standing on the water, calling her forward. The invitation wasn't to understand—but to trust.

Trina knew: stepping out was where provision met purpose.

A Prayer for Provision and Trust

Father God, thank You for showing that provision isn't something we earn—it's something we receive. Teach us to trust You when life doesn't make sense. Give us the courage to step out of the boat when You call us. Remind us that Your plans are good, Your heart is kind, and Your ways are perfect.

I pray for the one reading now—that they would see You move. That You'd bring provision in unexpected ways. That friends would come alongside them, as You did for Trina. That the flowers in their life would bloom again. May they walk forward with boldness, faith, and peace, knowing You hold their future.

In Jesus' mighty and powerful Name and through the power of the Holy Spirit,

Amen.

Being Vulnerable & Entering in Prayer

After stepping out in faith, where provision met purpose, Trina learned something deeper: God's goal wasn't just to make her comfortable. It was to make her holy. She remembered the words from James 1:4: *"Let perseverance finish its work so that you may be mature and complete, not lacking anything."*

Provision was not simply about meeting needs—it was about shaping her character.

One morning, overwhelmed by anxiety after moving yet again, Trina sat on the edge of her bed. Tears welled up in her eyes. "Why can't I just be settled?" she whispered. It was then she felt the gentle nudge in her spirit: *"Cast all your cares on Me, because I care for you."*—1 Peter 5:7.

It wasn't about finding another place to live—it was about learning to surrender. God wasn't punishing her with instability; He was inviting her to trust. He wanted her to stop trying to earn peace and simply receive it.

The process was uncomfortable, but Trina knew God was calling her higher—not just into a new apartment, but into maturity. Into wholeness.

In those quiet moments, Trina stopped praying for just an answer. She prayed to be transformed. The cry of her heart shifted:

"Father, make me holy, not just happy. Teach me to grow, not just get by. Complete what You've started in me." The Bible says, "the testing of our faith produces perseverance." He truly wants us to be made whole and one way is to cast our cares unto the Lord.

What does it really mean to *"cast all your anxiety on Him, because He cares for you"*?

For Trina, it meant learning to let go. And that wasn't easy. She was used to carrying everything herself. Fear had been her constant companion. Trust felt impossible. But when God truly entered her life, she slowly realized: she didn't have to carry it all. He was inviting her to set it down.

She wasn't alone. She was created on purpose, for a purpose.

Ephesians 2:10 became her reminder: *"For we are God's masterpiec*

He has created us anew in Christ Jesus, so we can do the good things He planned for us long ago."

But embracing this truth required something from her: vulnerability. Trust. And prayer.

In her early months in San Diego, Trina was attending a church where faith wasn't just talked about—it was demonstrated. People spoke of faith moving mountains. Mark 11:23 felt less like poetry and more like an invitation: *"...but shall believe in his heart that what he saith will come to pass, he will have what he saith."*

With her whole heart, Trina prayed: "God, please show me who You really are."

Time after time, He answered—not always in ways she expected, but always in ways she needed. She remembered her past. The moments God had carried her. The quiet ways He had proven Himself faithful.

Trust, she learned, wasn't a feeling. It was a choice. And she chose it—sometimes minute by minute.

Even when her circumstances said otherwise.

There were days when she felt abandoned—like the night she found herself packing her things after a landlord's deception left her without a home. Fear crept in as she moved her belongings into a friend's RV for the night. It seemed like life had fallen apart.

But it hadn't. Not in God's eyes.

Through mentorship and wise counsel—something Scripture encourages over and over (Proverbs 11:14, 1 Thessalonians 5:11)—she found the strength to hope again. She posted online, trusting her gut, believing that somehow, provision was waiting.

And it was. She knew it was God.

The very next day, a man responded to her inquiry: a small studio, behind a home in Cardiff-by-the-Sea. Private entrance. Affordable. Near the ocean.

Trina's heart overflowed with gratitude. God had provided more than shelter—He had given her peace.

As she settled into her new space, she realized something deeper: her identity wasn't as someone waiting for the worst. She was someone meant to *expect* the best. Not because life was perfect, but because God was trustworthy.

Even in the scams she faced—the bounced checks during COVID, the riddle scam on Facebook—God reminded her: *"Don't dwell. I'm your Father. I know what you need."*

And through it all, Trina learned the rhythm of vulnerability: bringing her needs to God in prayer, and letting His peace hold her.

A Prayer of Vulnerability

Father God, We exalt You. We surrender to You. Through every circumstance—through every loss, confusion, or unexpected moment—speak to us. Teach us that Your nearness is the answer we've been searching for.

Re-align our hearts. Re-awaken our trust. Re-center our lives in You. May every situation lead us back to Your presence. May every setback teach us to rely on You—not our strength, not our plan, not our understanding. You are the Author of our story.

Teach us to enter into Your presence not with polished prayers, but with vulnerable hearts. And may we, like Trina, discover that trust is not a feeling—but a daily choice to say: "I choose You, Lord."

In Jesus' mighty and powerful name, through the power of the Holy Spirit,

Amen.

This is YOUR Identity

Vulnerability often feels like weakness, but in the Kingdom of God, it's the first doorway to strength. After all, only when we lay down the walls we've built can God begin to show us who we truly are. For Trina, learning to be vulnerable with God meant opening the deepest parts of herself—the confusion, the fear, the aching desire to feel seen, known, and loved without conditions. And it was in those surrendered moments that He whispered her true identity.

The Lord was not asking her to strive to become someone else. He was calling her back to who He said she already was: His daughter. Chosen. Beloved. Redeemed. This is where the healing begins—not in doing more, but in believing more.

"I have hidden your Word in my heart that I might not sin against you."
—Psalm 119:11

We often strive for worthiness when God's Word simply invites us to abide in it. His promises are not something we earn, but something we receive. Temptations to doubt, fear, and believe the enemy's lies come easily, but Trina learned to pray for discernment: to ask God to expose the subtle strategies of the enemy. As Ephesians 6:12-13 reminds us:

"For our struggle is not against flesh and blood but against the rulers, against authorities, against the powers of this dark world and against spiritual forces of evil in the heavenly realms. Therefore put on the full armor of God so that when the day comes, you may be able to stand your ground, after you have done everything, to stand."

Trina understood now that identity is warfare. You don't defend what you don't value. So, day after day, she equipped herself—praying God's Word over her life, declaring truth against the voice of fear, and taking up the **shield of faith** that, as Scripture says, extinguishes every fiery dart of the enemy. When shame, fear, doubt, or accusation came, she reminded herself: "I lift the shield of faith. I block, absorb, and extinguish every negative word, lie, or attack that comes against my faith in who God says I am."

And as she walked forward, no longer striving for approval, she rested in the truth:

She was already approved. She was already called.

This identity in Christ was not about perfection—it was about connection. The more Trina leaned into God's presence, the more she saw Him as the Source of her peace, the Provider of her needs, and the Shepherd who would never leave her wandering.

God didn't call her to be productive before she could be loved. He called her loved so she could be fruitful.

The Joy of the Lord in the Small Things

Trina had learned that joy is not found in grand milestones, but in God's daily fingerprints—the quiet proof that He sees, He cares, and He provides. After stepping into vulnerability and her identity as a daughter of God, Trina discovered something deeper: **when you trust who He is, you start to see His love show up in the little things.**

For eleven years in San Diego, joy wove its way through every detail of her life. Though there were moments she had no idea where provision would come from, God never failed. Rent was always paid. Meals always appeared. Even lentils and hairspray—a grocery bag of answered prayer—showed up at her door from a neighbor. Oh, and one time for a year she didn't buy clothes but she wanted 5 specific things and her friend in Hawaii sent them to her! It was a joyous thing to experience after getting over her shopaholic days!

When she had no lunch, she'd pray: "Lord, I know You'll provide." Without fail, someone would offer her food. Her quiet refrain wherever she went became: **"Wherever I am, good things happen."** Since she had started believing in a God who delights to meet needs—big and small. She didn't ever take things for granted. Always giving credit to God for putting it on someone else to bless her. It was the simplest joy in her life.

She saw similar times of joy when she was scammed out of a rental and a friend named Joe opened his home. She saw again when a simple prayer for groceries was answered through a neighbor's kindness. Each moment was an invitation from God: "See how I care for you?" The groceries were exactly what she needed! It was uncanny how God sent even hairspray through a neighbor giving her food from Trader Joes!

Her life echoed Matthew 7:11:

"The lush generosity of God knows no limits."

And joy kept showing up. Trina once pictured a cabin in her prayer time—festive, cozy, Christmassy—and weeks later, she found herself invited to dog-sit in a cabin identical to her vision. Another time, she set a fleece before

God, asking for $300 flights to Hawaii—and He answered. These were not coincidences; they were love letters.

Joy in the small things is the evidence of His nearness.

But joy also grew from surrender. One day, while driving and feeling burdened by life's pressures, Trina heard the Lord whisper, **"Jesus already carried the Cross."** She realized she was carrying battles that weren't hers to fight. His reminder freed her to rest, knowing: the battle belongs to the Lord.

Abraham waited twenty-five years. Jacob, twenty. Joseph, thirteen. Moses, forty. All of them learned what Trina was learning: in the waiting and trials, God is forming endurance. As Dr. Paul Cho wrote, "Sometimes God wants to stiffen and strengthen up that backbone, and sometimes while being strengthened, you can almost hear the bones cracking." The small victories were teaching her spiritual endurance.

Joy wasn't just a byproduct—it was her strength.

Each smile. Each surprise meal. Each provision.

All of it was God's quiet declaration: "I am with you."

And when doubt whispered, she remembered Josiah. Her friend who'd been abandoned at birth and raised by adoptive parents. His mother would tell him, "God has engraved your name in the palm of His hand." Isaiah 49:16 confirmed it:

"See, I have inscribed you on the palms of My hands."

Every prayer whispered, every tear cried, every provision received—was known to God.

Trina's story, like Josiah's, became living proof:

You are never forgotten. You are held.

So, when life felt like a desert, joy became her oasis.

Each answered prayer in the small things was a reminder: God wasn't just sustaining her life—He was enriching it.

Can you remember a time when the Lord surprised you with a moment of joy—a blessing you didn't realize that God was blessing you? Close your eyes if you have a little time to have Him reveal it to you.

Here I Am, Mentality

Trina learned to carry a simple but powerful prayer in her heart: "Here I am, Lord." She came to understand that standing still before God—with an open heart and surrendered spirit—was not a sign of weakness, but of trust. After all, the battle belongs to the Lord, and the victory is His. Bringing a "Here I am" posture to God is an invitation for Him to move. It's about meeting Him exactly where you are, whether in a moment of peace, confusion, or exhaustion.

One day, while driving, Trina heard the gentle whisper of God: "Jesus already carried the cross." That moment hit her deeply. She realized she had been carrying burdens that were never hers to carry—worries, fears, false responsibilities. She had been holding onto crosses that Jesus had already taken up for her. And in that moment, peace began to settle her heart.

Throughout scripture, Trina reflected, God's people endured long seasons of testing: Abraham waited twenty-five years to see his promise fulfilled. Jacob endured hardship for twenty years. Joseph was enslaved and imprisoned for thirteen. Moses wandered forty years in the wilderness. The disciples faced lifelong trials. Waiting wasn't punishment. It was preparation.

She remembered reading in *The Fourth Dimension* by Dr. Paul Cho: "Do not throw your hands up in defeat and cry, 'Oh, where is God?' God is always there, and He is testing you. Sometimes God wants to stiffen and strengthen up that backbone, and sometimes while being strengthened, you can almost hear the bones cracking."

Trina knew the discomfort of waiting seasons. She often wondered how and when things would change. But she wasn't doubting God's presence—she was learning to shift her focus. Instead of stress, she began declaring God's Word over her life. She started praying not only for herself but for others who, like her, were burdened and weary.

What helped her most was realizing: *we are limited.* God never intended for her to carry life's weight alone. She had to tell herself daily: *Speak life. Speak the Word. Speak truth.* She learned to guide her mind and body with her own words, shaping her internal world by speaking aloud God's promises.

Jesus had already told His followers to expect difficulties:

"In this world, you will have trouble. But take heart! I have overcome the world." —John 16:33

Rather than succumbing to fear or deception, Trina examined her heart:

Do I trust God? Yes or no?

In those quiet reflections, she remembered Jesus' warning: "Do not be deceived." The enemy works through familiar strategies—lies, discouragement, fear. Like a roaring lion, Satan seeks those he can devour (1 Peter 5:8). But knowing this, Trina stood alert, steady in faith.

Because those who *fight in faith* are the ones who *rest in trust.*

Her journey wasn't just her own. In one season, Trina met Josiah, a gentle soul on the autism spectrum who regularly bought products from her online store. Over shared meals, he opened his heart to her. He told her how, as an abandoned infant, he was left in a hospital trash bin. Adopted as a baby, he struggled with feelings of rejection. His mother comforted him throughout his childhood by reciting Isaiah 49:16: "See, I have inscribed you on the palms of My hands."

She reminded him: You are never forgotten. Not by me. And never by God.

That image stayed with Trina. Like a mother who tattoos her children's names onto her skin, God had engraved her name on His very hands. No matter how forgotten or overlooked she felt, she was secure in His love.

The "Here I Am" mentality taught her to stand still—and stand secure. No striving. No performing. Just surrendering to the God who had already written her name in His story.

Father God, thank You for the simple joys that remind us You are near. Thank You for every moment of provision, every unexpected blessing, and every small reminder that You care for us in both ordinary and extraordinary ways. Help us to slow down, to notice, and to treasure each moment of grace You place in our lives. Teach us to live with open hands and grateful hearts, knowing that even our daily needs matter to You. Fill us with the joy that comes from knowing You are our Provider and Sustainer. Help us to carry this joy into every part of our lives, sharing it freely with others. In Jesus' mighty and powerful name and through the power of the Holy Spirit,

Amen.

Reflective Question:

Have you ever paused to ask God to help you remember the joyful moments He has already given you? Could it be that He has been faithful in more ways than you've yet seen? Take time now to ask Him to show you.

Source of Life

The thing is... this is coming from the One who has conquered it all. When we say that, we're acknowledging there is a Source of life outside of the natural realm. He is supernatural. He is made of love—and He longs to communicate with us. What a relief. Think about that. He's not too busy. He isn't distracted. The One who upholds the universe by the word of His power has time for you.

Trina entered a season of deep, anchored faith—a kind of faith that grew from knowing God personally, not theoretically. God showed her *Deuteronomy 28:47*, reminding her that joy in serving Him is essential. Then one day, while worshipping to the song *Way Maker*, God whispered something so simple yet so profound: "That is who I am." Way Maker. Miracle Worker. Promise Keeper. Light in the Darkness.

Deuteronomy 26:16-19 confirmed His heart:

"This day the Lord your God commands you to do these statutes and rules. You shall, therefore, be careful to do them with all your heart and with all your soul... And the Lord has declared today that you are a people for his treasured possession... and that you shall be a people holy to the Lord your God, as He promised."

Trina realized it didn't matter how her circumstances looked. God could be trusted as the healer of all situations. She wouldn't always be able to change her surroundings, but she could choose to be changed within them. She had been walking her faith journey for years, striving to "do her best." But then God showed her something new: grace is not earned; it's received.

Why could she receive this grace? Because Jesus made the way.

Jesus, who knew no sin, became sin for us (2 Corinthians 5:21). Though He was blameless, He took on guilt and condemnation so we could be absolved. He bore the punishment we deserved. God used His perfect Son to redeem His imperfect children. Through the cross, Jesus became the bridge that allows us to be seen as righteous before God—fully forgiven, fully accepted.

In those quiet moments, Trina began to believe: even when betrayed, abandoned, or misunderstood, she could trust that God's love was protecting her. That His ways—even when unseen—were always good.

She remembered *Romans 8:28*: "We know that in all things God works for the good of those who love Him, who have been called according to His purpose." Even when she didn't see it, even when it didn't make sense—He never stopped working.

In the lyrics of *Way Maker*:

"Even when I don't see it, You're working.

Even when I don't feel it, You're working.

You never stop. You never stop working."

This was who God is.

From the devotional *Growing in Grace* by Paul Tsika, she was reminded:

"It's hard to know who to trust when everything around us feels unstable. But God? He's different. He's the One who keeps His promises."

And the promises are many:

- He who began a good work will carry it to completion (Philippians 1:6).

- He will never leave you nor forsake you (Deuteronomy 31:8).

- Draw near to Him, and He will draw near to you (James 4:8).

- Trust in Him with all your heart, and He will direct your steps (Proverbs 3:5-6).

Trina began to rest—not in the world's guarantees but in God's eternal faithfulness.

Prayer:

Father God, Thank You for being my Source of life and hope. Thank You for sending Jesus—the One who knew no sin yet bore my sin, who died so I could live free. Teach me to trust You more deeply, to surrender control, and to receive Your grace with open hands. Let me find rest in knowing You are always working for my good, even when I cannot see it. Lead me to experience Your love daily, and help me remember that You are not just my Provider, but my Father. In Jesus' Mighty and powerful Name and through the power of the Holy Spirit.

Amen.

An Eternal Mindset

Trina had to learn what it meant to live with an eternal mindset. She needed to press into the nature of Who God is—a Father of all-encompassing love. In every area of her life, He wanted to help her. She realized someone the reasons why: too much was at stake. Her value. Her purpose. Her identity. In her weakness she was given strength to persevere and see that Only God, the Restorer of all things, could bring life back into places that felt dead. She started to believe it: if she wasn't moving forward, she was sliding backward. Not because she was failing—but because she was designed to grow an lean on Him. God created us to be "forward-thinkers" in a spiritual sense.

It reminded her of Paul's words in *Philippians 3:13-14*: "Forgetting what is behind and straining toward what is ahead, I press on toward the goal to win the prize for which God has called me heavenward in Christ Jesus." Trina felt this deep in her spirit: life with God meant forward thinking—not clinging to past regrets, but stepping forward in faith toward His promises.

Isaiah 43:18-19 echoed this: "Forget the former things; do not dwell on the past. See, I am doing a new thing!" God was inviting her to trust again.

Trina learned that scrutinizing every detail of her life wasn't helpful. She didn't need to control every expense, every conversation, every outcome. She needed to trust that God had His hand over her because she was seeking His will—especially through community. She started giving herself more grace, knowing she couldn't miss God's plan if she stayed in His presence.

She had prayed one morning, on her drive to the job she once thought was her "dream career" in HR:

"God, if this isn't the right opportunity, take it away. I trust You."

That day, She lost the position—but gained a life of freedom. Working as a simple hostess, humbling herself with every guest she seated, she found joy in serving. She worked with integrity, even when she wondered, *"Why am I here? I could be doing so much more."* Yet she felt peace. God was stripping away her pride and giving her something better: purpose rooted in His presence.

Even when her living situation suddenly changed, and she had to leave a place she loved, she prayed through the frustration:

"Father God, help. I'm confused and tired. I trust You to lead me."

She began showing up for church again, leaning into Christian friendships, realizing that loving others, pursuing healing, and letting go of fear was far more valuable than anything her career could offer. She didn't need to scrutinize everything—she needed to trust Him.

Her days started to fill with simple prayers:

- *"Lord, teach me to be present in the lives of others."*

- *"God, show me who You want me to see today."*

- *"Help me see beyond my phone. Help me focus. Help me live in the now." "Jesus, make me Your vessel. Use me."*

Over time, she understood: her purpose wasn't complicated. Her calling was clear. She was to love. To serve. To be a light.

As John 13:35 said: "By this everyone will know that you are my disciples, if you love one another."

That's when it clicked. This life was about loving Him, and loving others as He did. Over and over, Trina had met people who didn't get that. Friendships and relationships fell apart because they were centered on superficial goals, not the heart of God.

But she wasn't meant to shrink back. She was meant to become a spiritual lioness—strong, bold, willing to go through difficulty to proclaim that there is a Father in Heaven who wants to heal, protect, and raise His children into warriors.

She remembered her earliest days in San Diego, when everything had fallen apart. A family friend had tried to send her back home after her job offer disappeared. She could have gone—but God had something better. Through strangers, random encounters, and divine provision, He kept opening doors. Little did she know, those 30 days of holding onto hope would prepare her for the life of faith ahead.

Looking back, she realized her greatest victories didn't come from striving. They came from surrender.

An Eternal Mindset means trusting God enough to stop overthinking—and start abiding.

Prayer for an Eternal Mindset

Father God, Thank You for being patient with me when I struggle to trust You. Teach me what it means to think forward—not trapped in the past, but stepping boldly into the future You've prepared for me. Help me release the urge to control every detail, and instead rest in Your presence and plans.

I ask for grace in the places where I've been hard on myself. I ask for courage when I fear moving forward. Shape me, Lord, into someone who sees each challenge as an invitation to grow closer to You. Help me see my life as You do—not wasted, not behind, but right on time.

You promise in *Philippians 1:6* that You will complete the good work You've begun in me. I stand on that promise today. Help me walk forward, step by step, trusting You with what's ahead.

I surrender my life, my plans, and my identity to You. Use me, Father, for Your glory.

In Jesus' mighty and powerful name,

Amen.

So Much Joy in the Journey

Trina had learned a simple yet profound truth: knowing her limitations wasn't failure—it was an invitation. When she recognized her own limitations, she could finally ask God to provide her with what she needed. It wasn't weakness to admit she couldn't have all the energy or even financial ability; it was wisdom to ask Him. She knew that she needed to learn to rely on God and have some delayed gratification. It wasn't deprivation—it was training. She was being shown how He could move with anything she needed. Wisdom itself was a blessing from God, guiding her not to overspend, not to chase after what culture said she needed, but to see how trusting Him to provide in due season led to understanding. More importantly, she could address the reasons leading her to have issues with controlling her spending.

She came to see that biblical prosperity extended far beyond finances. It encompassed spiritual peace, physical provision to have healing, emotional stability with peace and joy, and soul deep joy regardless of her circumstances. God's character was rich in grace, mercy, love, and faithfulness—and those were the true riches she began to seek. As Scripture encourages, contentment with life's basic needs wasn't settling for less; it was recognizing that the greatest wealth is a life rooted in relationship with God.

Scripture reinforced this lesson again and again. Proverbs 19:8 became her quiet anchor:

"Do yourself a favor and learn all you can; then remember what you learn and you will prosper."

It wasn't just about knowledge, though. It was about humility. About saying, *Lord, I don't know everything—but You do.*

God's Word offered other wisdom to steward life with trust:

- **Proverbs 11:25** – "Be generous and you will prosper. Help others, and you will be helped."

- **Proverbs 19:17** – "When you give to the poor, it is like lending to the Lord, and the Lord will repay you."

- **Proverbs 21:5** – "Plan carefully and you will have plenty; act too quickly and you will never have enough."

For Trina, prosperity was no longer about money—it was about the richness of God's presence. True wealth, she realized, was walking in step with the One who held her life. Her treasure wasn't stored in a bank account; it was stored in a heart increasingly shaped by grace.

She remembered laughing once at a story—a woman at a gym had picked up a phone left behind on a bench, answering it without hesitation. On the other end, a man, mistaking her for his wife, unknowingly authorized extravagant purchases: a mink coat, a luxury car, even beachfront property. After the call ended, the woman casually asked the locker room, "Does anyone know whose phone this is?"

The lesson stayed with Trina: who you're consulting matters.

In life, she knew she couldn't afford to listen to the wrong voices. Her decisions couldn't be based on assumption or impulse. She needed the counsel of the One who knew her heart and saw the path ahead.

So she sought the Lord's voice first. Not out of fear—but out of trust. As her pastor once said, "God's priority is closeness. Provision follows relationship."

She reflected often on **Acts 17:24–28**:

"The God who made the world and everything in it is the Lord of heaven and earth... He himself gives everyone life and breath and everything else... God did this so that they would seek Him and perhaps reach out for Him and find Him, though He is not far from any one of us. For in Him we live and move and have our being."

God wasn't distant. He wasn't withholding. He was the Source of life itself.

Trina also came to cherish the truth of **2 Corinthians 5:21**:

"God made Him who knew no sin to be sin for us, so that in Him we might become the righteousness of God."

Jesus' sacrifice meant she was already approved, already loved, already provided for. She didn't need to scrutinize every detail of her life. She could rest in grace, anchored in community, seeking God's will. His hand was over her life. His promises are secure. He cannot lie.

As Proverbs 16:20 promised:

"Those who listen to instruction will prosper; those who trust the Lord will be happy."

Day by day, as she walked out her journey, Trina no longer chased material wealth or earthly validation. She chased wisdom. She sought the Lord's face.

And in that pursuit, she discovered joy—not just in the answered prayers, but in the waiting, the learning, and the slow, steady becoming.

Her joy was no longer circumstantial. It was rooted in something deeper: contentment in God Himself.

Father God, Thank You for showing us that true prosperity is not measured by what we own, but by knowing You. Help us, like Trina, to recognize our limitations as invitations to trust You more deeply. Teach us the joy of waiting, the strength of contentment, and the blessing of walking in step with Your wisdom. Let Your grace and provision remind us daily that You are not distant—you are near, and You are faithful. In the mighty and powerful name of Jesus.

Amen.

Generosity Spirit Wins

"The generous prosper and are satisfied; those who refresh others will themselves be refreshed." — *Proverbs 11:25*

For Trina, generosity wasn't just an act—it had become a way of life. She had learned that blessing others wasn't about how much she had in her hand, but about how open her heart was. The more she gave—her time, her attention, her compassion, and her resources—the more her soul felt full. Not full because of applause or recognition, but because she was walking in rhythm with the God who is, by His very nature, generous.

She often said, *"We are blessed to be a blessing."* It wasn't just a saying—it was her mindset. She lived with the conviction that God's abundance wasn't meant to be hoarded but shared. Whether it was paying for someone's coffee, giving away clothes she loved, or encouraging someone with words soaked in kindness, Trina believed that a generous spirit always wins.

She remembered seasons when she didn't have much. And yet—somehow—there was always enough. Someone would drop off groceries. A friend would surprise her with gas money. An unexpected check would arrive in the mail. Each moment was a whisper from God: *I see you. I'll take care of you. Keep pouring out—I'll keep pouring in.*

True generosity, she realized, wasn't about wealth. It was about trust. Trust that God, as the Source, would always refill what she released.

Her heart was drawn to the words of 2 Corinthians 9:8:

"And God is able to bless you abundantly, so that in all things at all times, having all that you need, you will abound in every good work."

Generosity wasn't just about money. It was giving grace when someone didn't deserve it. It was choosing kindness instead of criticism. It was letting love lead, even when life felt tight.

Trina often reflected on this truth: when we give freely, we reflect the heart of Jesus—the One who gave all. His generosity on the cross wasn't deserved. It wasn't partial. It was complete. And because He gave, we can live.

In a world that tells us to hold tightly, hoard, and secure, Trina chose the better way. The Kingdom way. The way of overflow.

Prayer:

Father God, You are the most generous Giver of all. You gave us life, breath, and most of all—Your Son. Help me to reflect Your heart in how I give. Let my hands be open, not clenched. Teach me to refresh others, not for reward, but because it delights You.

Show me the opportunities to sow love, time, kindness, and resources, even in seasons when I feel stretched. I trust that You will always provide, and I ask for a spirit of joyful generosity that honors You in every area of my life.

Let my life be a river, not a reservoir. Use me, Lord, as a vessel of blessing. In Jesus' mighty and powerful name,

Amen.

The Freedom of Forgiveness

We've all been there. Holding hope for something—a relationship, an opportunity, a dream—only to watch it slip through our fingers. For Trina, disappointment wasn't unfamiliar. She had placed her hope in people, in plans that seemed secure, in futures that felt so close she could touch them. But when things unraveled, the harder part wasn't just accepting the loss—it was learning to trust herself again.

Forgiveness, she discovered, wasn't only about others. Sometimes, the person we need to forgive most... is ourselves.

She remembered the countless seasons where confusion wrapped around her heart like a heavy fog. She longed for stability, for a family, for a love that cherished her for who she was. Yet, again and again, disappointment forced her to dig deep into the roots of her insecurity.

And yet, even in the midst of unmet expectations, joy was still possible. She had to choose it. Day after day. Step after trembling step.

Trina realized that every moment of brokenness held a deeper invitation: to believe that nothing was wasted. Each closed door, each painful goodbye, each unanswered prayer—they weren't punishments. They were lessons. Lessons to teach her discernment. Lessons to teach her that God's "no" often meant "I have something better."

Forgiving herself wasn't a weakness. It was maturity. It was giving herself permission to acknowledge: *What I hoped for mattered. What I lost hurt. But God is not done with me.*

She learned to release regret, to surrender shame, and to keep her heart open to hope. Her story wasn't over.

And neither is yours.

You weren't created to settle. Disappointment isn't your identity. Your dreams, your God-given aspirations—they matter. The pain you've walked through doesn't disqualify you; it qualifies you to trust in a deeper way. Keep believing. Stay in faith. Live in a bubble of love. You are being shaped, not sidelined.

As Trina reminded herself daily: *Every disappointment is a doorway to a greater promise.*

Prayer:

Father God, You see every disappointment I carry. You know the silent grief I've tried to ignore, the broken hopes I've buried. Thank You for reminding me that none of it is wasted. Teach me to forgive—not just those who hurt me—but myself. Show me how to release regret and step into trust again.

Help me believe You're writing a better story. Heal my heart where it feels fragile. Replace fear with faith. May I never stop hoping, never stop dreaming, never stop believing that You are good—and that Your plans for me are still unfolding.

In Jesus' Mighty and Powerful Name,

Amen.

When Things Are Confusing: Now Faith

For Trina, learning to trust in the midst of confusion wasn't just a lesson; it became a way of life. When plans unraveled—when what she thought would work didn't—she discovered the quiet strength of *Now Faith*. As Hebrews 11:1 reminds us, "Now faith is confidence in what we hope for and assurance about what we do not see."

In those moments when fear whispered louder than hope, the temptation was to analyze, overthink, and control outcomes. But Trina came to understand that faith isn't about seeing—it's about trusting. And trust meant releasing control.

As Jordan Lee Dooley writes in *Embrace Your Almost*, "I didn't see it in that frustrating and stressful moment, but I see it now: in those back-to-back experiences that forced me to replan a year twice within the first quarter, I was learning how to release control in ways I hadn't had to before."

For Trina, that meant learning to say, "I have the mind of Christ." 1 Corinthians 2:16 promises this reality: "But we have the mind of Christ." Philippians 2:5 calls believers to "Let this mind be in you, which was also in Christ Jesus." His mind was one of surrender, trust, and perfect obedience to the Father. Trina realized she was being invited to think differently—not as the world taught her, but as Christ would have her.

Delays weren't denials. Setbacks weren't failures. They were invitations: opportunities to let go and let God.

It wasn't easy. After months of job hunting and rejection, after being asked awkward questions in interviews about why nothing seemed to work out, she had to face her own disappointment. But rather than give in to despair, Trina chose to believe that God's plan hadn't been canceled—only recalibrated. Her battle wasn't in hustling harder; her battle was in prayer, faith, and surrender.

She remembered Joseph—the dreamer loved by his father yet betrayed by his brothers. Even in prison, Joseph chose to believe in God's future for him. And eventually, he found favor with a king.

Like Joseph, Trina realized that favor comes not from human plans but from trusting God's hand. She was learning to pray more, worry less, and believe that every detour could still lead to destiny.

Now, when life grew confusing, Trina learned to pause and declare:

I have the mind of Christ.

I will trust You, God, even here.

And in those moments, peace returned.

Prayer:

Father God, When life is confusing and plans crumble, help me remember that I have the mind of Christ. Quiet the noise of fear, and replace it with Your peace. Help me trust that Your ways are higher, even when I cannot understand them. Give me the courage to release control and to find rest in surrender. May Your voice be the one I follow, even when the path feels unclear. *Let Now Faith* arise within me—the faith to trust You here, now, in this very moment.

In Jesus' mighty and powerful name,

Amen.

When Forgiveness Is Not About You

Each day, Trina realized that what she saw as her personal "issue" often wasn't the real problem. The real issue was the emotion holding her captive—the unresolved hurt, the fear, the disappointment—that stalled her growth. She remembered a time when joy came easily. Now, it felt distant. But what she began to understand was this: everything she had walked through—the confusion, the setbacks, the disappointments—had all led her to this moment. And if she could choose to see it, even the pain had a purpose.

There's peace in knowing that nothing is wasted in God's hands. Even what feels like a failure can become part of His refining work in you. But there's a key truth we must embrace: taking authority over your life isn't about controlling every outcome—it's about choosing agreement with what God is doing, even when it doesn't make sense.

Trina began to understand that every negative circumstance had, in some mysterious way, brought her closer to Him. It had grown her. Strengthened her. And softened her heart to depend not on herself, but on the One who knew her future.

The key to open every locked door? Sharing your life with Him.

Her pastor once said something simple, yet life-changing: *"God doesn't just want obedience. He wants relationship. He wants you to know how deeply He loves you."*

That truth could carry her through anything.

She found comfort in Jeremiah 33:2–3, even when she felt confined, like Jeremiah himself in the courtyard of the guard:

"This is what the Lord says, he who made the earth, the Lord who formed it and established it—the Lord is his name: 'Call to me, and I will answer you and tell you great and unsearchable things you do not know.'"

Even though perilous times were coming, God's mercy remained:

"'Nevertheless, I will bring health and healing to it; I will heal my people and let them enjoy abundant peace and security. I will cleanse them from all the sin they have committed against me and forgive all their sins of rebellion against me... And they will be in awe and tremble at the abundant prosperity and peace I provide for it.'"

God had a plan to rebuild. To restore. To forgive.

And in this, Trina realized something even deeper about forgiveness: **it wasn't just about her**. When God forgives us, it's not because we deserve it—it's because of His nature. His love. His grace. And when He calls us to forgive others, it's not about keeping score or waiting for an apology. It's about releasing ourselves from the chains of bitterness.

Forgiveness frees us—not just the other person.

She remembered Romans 4:7:

"Blessed are those whose transgressions are forgiven, whose sins are covered."

Trina could rest in knowing her sins were covered. And she could extend that grace to others, not from her own strength, but from the mercy she herself had received.

A Prayer for This Moment

Father God, Thank You for loving us first. Thank You for sending Jesus—not just to model forgiveness, but to be forgiveness itself. He who knew no sin became sin for us, so we could be free. Lord, we confess we don't always understand how to let go, how to move forward, or how to forgive ourselves and others. But today, we choose to trust You. Cover us in Your mercy. Wash us in Your peace. Fill us with joy, not because circumstances are perfect, but because You are with us in every circumstance. Thank You for giving us the grace to grow. May we see the doors You are opening, and may we be willing to step through them.

In Jesus' mighty and powerful name and through the power of the Holy Spirit,

Amen.

Wisdom

Trina was able to spend a great amount of time with God. She felt so blessed and honored for the time she could sit with Him. She sat on a yoga mat in her backyard, just meditating on images that the Lord had given to her. Later, she had a pink chair to sit on where she could hear from God. It was the best way to really come humbly before the throne of grace and mercy as it says in Hebrews 4:16. Not sitting in her bed though or else she'd fall asleep. She felt the value of keeping the 10 Commandments was very important. He wants us to accept Jesus as our Savior, to follow the 10 commandments because it's helping us live in freedom. It's not about legalism. He wants us to be free as God's people. Free life of the Israelites when they were captive as slaves for 430 years. To remind us that people learn who they were meant to be and to begin living a new life. He wants us to have physical freedom, from sickness, emotional freedom too. In Romans 8:18, the mindset is we have to consider our present sufferings are not worth comparing with the glory that will be revealed in us.

If you were told to listen to God daily, and he would actually make big things happen in your life, would you do it? One day it says in Job 2:28, "And it shall come to pass afterward that I will pour out My Spirit on all flesh; You sons and your daughters shall prophesy. Your old men shall dream dreams, Your young men shall see visions."

Whether or not one of us steps into our purpose God will make a way for His way and glory to be known. The wickedness will not prevail.

Spending time with friends was the best thing she could do. She would work out with friends one day in Alpine, CA. There was a man who always posed the craziest questions.

Wisdom is shared this way. When you ask for one drink. His presence is satiating. Psalm 78: 15-16. He split open rock to provide water. Then, streams began to flow from them like rivers.

These verses remind us that God's power and care are never limited by our circumstances—He is always able to meet the needs of His people. Going back to Trina's guy friend who posed the most interesting questions. God uses women and men to help us think wisely and even just differently. Even though his question was about dating and how to have a woman say yes to a second date... he was helping his friends come to a realization that there is work to be done.

Grieving: Sometimes It Goes Like This

The Lord knows those who are faithful will seek Him. As Deuteronomy 4:29 promises, "But if from there you will seek the LORD your God, you will find Him if you seek Him with all your heart and with all your soul." Trina had to learn that firsthand. In her darkest moments, she discovered that grief itself could become a place of encounter.

There were days when the Lord seemed to invite her to cry out—to release the pain that tried to take root in her heart. Sometimes, grief felt like war. Sometimes we have to be gentle. Sometimes, we have to cast out thoughts that are not in alignment. Tell the enemy to get out! It's the enemy! That's why they can't see. It's with boldness that we intercede to leave His children alone.

He wants you to have peace with how it's all for a greater purpose. It says, "In grief or in mourning, it is all for the glory of God." He wants to be made known as your helper, comforter, and everything else! That means that you will have to surrender.

Being filled with the knowledge of God will give you peace as you surrender.

Surrendering is Bitter and Oh, SO Sweet!

Trina recalled moving multiple times and saying to God, "I literally physically give it to you, God." I really have seen the times when it was a phone call or a person that I spoke with that brought me to the realization that HE wants me to surrender it. As I continue to practice this, there are times when I believe He already is bringing what I wanted. I just have to trust. Know in the back of your mind that you will be in the right place at the right time. And that in the moment when you feel prompted, you will allow yourself to be led.

Prayer

Father God, I will keep praying until your answer comes. I declare that you have big plans for me. I will speak up in a loud voice knowing you hear us when we cry out to you. I am open to receive the wisdom you have for me as I fight back with wisdom and patience in this season. Even when it feels like war I will pray to get rid of my Ego and Pride. Our circumstances will change once we do. In the mighty and powerful name of Jesus and through the power of the Holy Spirit.

Amen.

A New Phase

Rejoice in the Morning!

"Your Word is a lamp to my feet and a light to my path." —Psalm *119:105*

Welcoming a "new you" rarely comes with a celebration. No announcement. No parade. Just a quiet shift.

You moved on. You grew. You transcended something that once held you back. And though there may be no trumpet sound, people *feel* it. They *notice*—you're not the person they once knew.

That is a big deal.

Be happy they noticed. It means something is truly changing.

Then comes the silence. You're no longer spending time with the same people. You find yourself making quiet exits, dodging old patterns, distancing from what once felt familiar.

We've *all* been there.

But this is where the Holy Spirit steps in—your Advocate. The One who gently convicts not to shame, but to **remind you who you are in Christ**: *righteous, redeemed, holy.* The Spirit helps you discern truth from lies—especially the accusing voice of the enemy.

If we don't intentionally **disassociate from that voice of condemnation**, it becomes much harder to hear the still, small voice of the Holy Spirit. The one leading you forward.

The best part of growth is the *renewal of your mind.*

New thinking. New habits. **New people.**

When you let go of your old self—your old ways of thinking—you make space for what's truly from God. These people you meet? These moments of clarity? They're no accident.

As we say in California, they're a **God-send.**

If you're in a season of building—business, calling, or healing—*every single minute matters.* When your time is focused and your intention clear, a single day can change everything.

But let me ask you:

- Is it really *up to you*?
- Are *your* efforts what will get you there?
- Do you truly hold the power over the moments that define your breakthrough?

The truth is, we act because we expect something to happen. We show up with faith. Because doing nothing produces nothing. But when we move in expectation—not striving—we partner with God.

Even now, I'm in a new season. I'm editing—and honestly, I'm grateful I skipped the glass of wine. I needed this clarity. This *momentum.*

And it hit me:

Maybe trusting *more* is what allows the flow.

Maybe when we let go, God takes us where we need to go—**in our minds and in our thoughts.**

Let's talk forgiveness.

For yourself. For others. You can't carry bitterness and expect to move forward in freedom.

You don't know what others are walking through—the burdens, the brokenness behind poor decisions. And you're not meant to judge it. You're meant to be free from the burdens.

There's a moment when you must *acknowledge the next right step*, not stay stuck in what went wrong.

"If we confess our sins, He is faithful and just to forgive us and cleanse us from all unrighteousness." —1 John 1:9

"You are blameless because you were made righteous."

We relate to one another because we *feel*—we cry, we laugh, we struggle, and sometimes we do it all at once while cooking dinner! That doesn't make me better than you. It just makes me real.

It's a fine line we walk between where we are and where we long to be.

But here's the encouragement:

Whether you're walking with full confidence or crawling with no expectations, **if you're moving forward in trust**, it will be *that much sweeter* when you get there.

Because you didn't rush it.

You didn't fake it.

You **trusted the process**.

Sometimes, joy in the morning doesn't come as laughter. Sometimes it comes as a quiet shift in the heart—a letting go of bitterness, a softening, a realization that even this was not wasted.

Stacy knew what it felt like to lose everything.

At one point, Stacy had stability—a steady job, a car, a place to call home, and a loving family in San Diego who would have done anything for her. But in a single moment, a devastating car accident changed everything. Her income vanished. Her vehicle was gone. Her home slipped away. Though her family would have embraced her with open arms, she couldn't bring herself to reach out. The weight of shame settled in. She felt like the crash hadn't just wrecked her car—it had wrecked her sense of identity, too.

So she stayed on the street.

But God wasn't done writing her story.

In Carlsbad, California, she met a man who owned a Shelby car shop—a teacher, of sorts. Not just in mechanics, but in life. He saw past her circumstances. He reminded her of her worth. He didn't preach at her—he *guided* her. And through that simple mentorship, Stacy's heart began to open again.

She found strength to forgive.

Not just others—her family, the people who let her down. But *herself.*

And maybe even more importantly, she forgave God.

Not because God had done anything wrong, but because she'd been holding pain and confusion in her heart. Questions that had never been answered. Anger that had never been acknowledged.

Through that healing process, God gave her something more lasting than money or a home: **He gave her peace.** And in that peace, she saw the light of morning.

Closing Prayer: Rejoicing in the New Day

Father God, Thank You for the quiet mornings where You remind me that I am not who I once was. Thank You for the transformation happening even when no one claps, and for the stillness that follows growth.

Lord, I confess the moments I've clung to old patterns, old voices, and old fears. But today, I receive Your grace. I choose to trust that You are doing something new in me—even when I don't fully understand it.

Help me embrace the silence not as loneliness, but as sacred space.

Let it be the place where I hear Your voice more clearly, where my identity is reaffirmed, and where joy takes root.

Forgive me for striving in my own strength.

Teach me to move forward not with anxiety, but with expectation—believing that You are already working on my behalf.

Surround me with people who point me back to You.

Renew my mind. Guard my heart.

And let Your joy truly be my strength.

I may have wept through the night, but this morning—*this very moment*—I rejoice.

Because You are faithful.

You are good.

And joy has come.

In Jesus' name,

Amen.

WHAT IS "THE PROCESS?"

When life grows quiet, it's often because the soul has stepped into a storm. In those moments, thoughts arise—interrupting the tension...surfacing from places buried deep. Jordan Lee Dooley, in her book Embrace Your Almost, captures the sacredness of these interruptions when she writes:

"I wonder whether perhaps some of those experiences were not merely inconveniences but also invitations to trust God and grow in a way I might otherwise have missed, had I still been under the illusion that if I just planned enough or did enough, I would maintain full control."

That invitation—to release control—is the beginning of the process. And for many, it becomes a holy epiphany, a threshold they longed for without even knowing.

Humans tend to put tremendous pressure on themselves. They strive. They overthink. They try to get ahead of what only God can reveal in time. For those seeking God in earnest, this process becomes more than personal development—it becomes a path toward purpose.

In truth, everything that happens can be used for learning, and nothing is accidental. Though it may seem that the road is shaped by one's own thoughts or manifestations, Scripture teaches otherwise. The path was written long before birth.

"Your eyes saw my unformed body;

All the days ordained for me were written in your book

Before one of them came to be.

How precious to me are your thoughts, God!

How vast is the sum of them!" —Psalm 139:16–17

This brings a person to ask: *How does one know the right path?*

Scripture responds simply and profoundly:

"In the way of righteousness there is life; along that path is immortality."
—Proverbs 12:28

The path to life is not paved with perfection but with righteousness—a surrendered heart, a soul willing to trust.

Still, the questions come:

Does God really care about individual lives?

What about the future?

What happens when others don't share the same convictions or spiritual awareness?

These questions are valid. They surface during the stillness and the chaos. But in the middle of overanalyzing and attempting to see 500 steps ahead, a whisper often meets the heart:

"Don't worry about it.

Leave it to Me.

I've got you.

I've planned it all out.

Just trust Me."

The Creator knows His creation intimately. Every background, every family, every gift, and every fall is accounted for in His story. Each person, no matter how flawed they feel, remains a vital part of the human narrative God is telling.

There's no need to perform or prove anything. Every striving moment, every doubt, every wound is met with the same invitation: *Let go.*

God still calls people *fearfully and wonderfully made.*

He still says, *"Before I formed you in the womb, I knew you."*

He still promises, *"I will never leave you nor forsake you."*

In that truth, an image begins to form. God's hand—extended. Present. Steady. The reader is invited to picture it, pause, and grab hold.

That hand won't let go.

Even if a person walks away, God holds fast. Even if they never return to this chapter, or this spiritual place again, He remains near. He still wants to hear from them. Still calls them *beloved.* Still whispers, *"Keep Me in your love."*

And just like that, the awakening begins.

Circumstances may not instantly shift. But something inside does. The pressure lifts. The heart steadies. The soul breathes.

Because it was never about the person holding everything together.

It was always about the God who never let go.

And in that truth, a new confidence arises—not because of what has been done, but because of who He is.

"I am able."

"I've got this."

Because **He's got me.**

And then, the unimaginable happened.

The man who had guided her passed away in Stacy's life. But before he left, he entrusted the Shelby shop to her. Stacy—once homeless and forgotten—became the owner of a business that people from around the world sought out.

She didn't just keep the shop running; she innovated. She created a unique part for Shelby cars that couldn't be found anywhere else. What began in pain became a product of excellence, a symbol of purpose born from process.

What the enemy meant for harm, God turned into glory.

And that is the beauty of *the process.*

About to Cry?

By human strength alone, people were never meant to be invincible. In fact, they were designed to reach the end of themselves so they would reach for something greater.

"Come to Me, all who are weary," Jesus said in Matthew 11:28, "and I will give you rest."

Anyone who desires to approach God must believe that He exists—and that He rewards those who earnestly seek Him.

He can restore every part of a life—mind, heart, purpose, identity. And sometimes, the tears that form come not from weakness, but from the *weight* of what it took to get here. No one sees it. No one fully understands. It can't even be explained. The road was filled with resistance at every turn.

But that's greatness for you.

Never mind—that's a topic for another book.

And yet, sometimes all a person needs to do is just one thing:

MAMBA.

Rest in peace, Kobe.

That man was a machine—relentless, focused, and deeply rooted in vision.

And so is every person who learns to pursue trust like a calling.

That's what this book is about.

Seeking the Trust built into the fabric of a person's being that calls them forward. It often begins with a whisper and then grows into clarity. Many have stood in front of that vision and whispered, *"Wow… I saw that when I was young. I saw myself becoming that. A leader. A creative. A nurturer. A builder. A boss."* Whether they say it aloud or just carry it in the quiet, the truth is—it's there. It's always been there.

Sometimes that vision includes people—family, community, a future team. And sometimes, the call feels strangely personal, as if everything is being focused inward for a reason. Either way, there's joy in beginning to live it out.

Perhaps that vision is not for applause but for peace.

To see something clearly, even before it arrives, is a gift.

Trina knew that gift well.

In one of the quietest and most formative seasons of her life, she turned to books. Not one or two, but whole stacks. For a year, she read constantly—sometimes seven to ten books at a time. She devoured wisdom, testimony, instruction. Her heart was searching, and through story after story, she was rebuilt from the inside out.

It wasn't just reading—it was *renewing*.

A path of growth had opened, and she walked it faithfully, page by page.

There is value in receiving. It's a key distinction: trusting God doesn't mean sitting in stillness forever. There's a time to rest, yes—but also a time to *respond*. Stillness can become stagnation if not tempered with action.

Many know that moment—the job loss, the crossroads, the unexpected pause. Recuperation is necessary. But it must be paired with listening. And after listening, *moving*.

As Andy Stanley wrote in *Visioneering*,

"It is very hypocritical to ask others to take risks we are not willing to take ourselves. If God has birthed a vision in you, it is only a matter of time until you will come upon the precipice of sacrifice."

This is where transformation begins.

If someone were sitting at home, uncertain of their next step, the question would not be: *"What can you do?"*

It would be: *"What is the one thing you feel led to do?"*

And if the answer is unclear, then the prayer becomes simple:

"God, what do You want me to do today? Where do You want me to go?"

Even if the answer is small—stay home, rest, read, reach out—it's sacred.

This is how the inner path of growth is formed.

And something begins to happen: the more someone listens and acts, the more aligned they become. They find themselves in divine moments—in stores, on trails, at events—unexpected opportunities for joy, encouragement, or service.

These moments rarely unfold as planned. And yet, every time, there's purpose.

Maybe they're uplifted.

Maybe they uplift someone else.

Either way, *they're awakened.*

This is the journey.

It might begin with tears. It might feel uncertain. But it becomes the soil for healing, for new joy, for divine appointments, for hidden hikes on coastal bluffs in La Jolla.

Each step builds confidence. Each conversation matters.

And in each encounter, the same invitation echoes:

"Add value. Be present. Trust Me."

Even 15 minutes of intentional reading in the morning can shift a life.

Even one walk into a new place with open eyes can uncover something holy.

That is the sacred rhythm of those who seek trust.

And trust, when truly lived out, becomes a life beyond what anyone could have scripted.

...Each step builds confidence. Each conversation matters.

And in each encounter, the same invitation echoes:

"Add value. Be present. Trust Me."

Even 15 minutes of intentional reading in the morning can shift your life.

Even one walk into a new place with open eyes can uncover something holy.

And if there's ever a doubt—if the path seems too tangled, the dream too delayed, or the heart too weary to believe again—let this truth settle in:

"I am the Lord, the God of all mankind. Is anything too hard for me?" — *Jeremiah 32:27*

There is no dream too far gone.

No life too fractured.

No calling is too complex.

Nothing is too hard for God.

That is the sacred rhythm of those who seek trust.

And trust, when truly lived out, becomes a life beyond what anyone could have scripted.

Be Perfected by Stepping Back

Let God mature you and love you.

There is something powerful about stepping back—not as a retreat, but as a repositioning. In stepping back, one creates space. Space for God to mature. Space for God to love. Space for transformation.

At times, the thoughts that enter the heart begin to echo what others are also sensing. It's no coincidence. Whether it's one voice or many, the alignment of thought reveals something deeper at work: **personal growth.** And when thoughts shift, so does the person.

When someone starts developing themselves—spiritually, mentally, emotionally—they're confronting something in their current state that is *meant to be changed.* Every area of life, from finances to relationships to self-worth, is driven by thought.

For example, the idea that one "needs more" is just that—a thought. "I need more food." "I don't have enough money." "I have to get away." But what if the thought was instead, *"I have enough."*

That one thought could stop someone from driving to the store for snacks they don't need because they suddenly remember—*there's plenty in the fridge at home.*

Thoughts shape beliefs. Beliefs shape words.

Words become actions.

Actions form habits.

Habits cement mindset.

Mindset becomes attitude.

And that attitude becomes a reflection of character.

And character? That forms a person's destiny.

So yes—something as simple as chips, tomatoes, and eggs can reveal a lot.

Francis P. Martin in *Hung by the Tongue* writes,

"Consider Jesus the Apostle and High Priest of our confession."

He compares Moses to Jesus. Moses, faithfully he often cried out to God because the people wore him down with their complaints, their unbelief. But now, Jesus is our High Priest—our go-between. And just like in the days of Moses, Jesus still hears the words His people speak.

Do those words weary Him too?

Words matter. They shape reality. "Words produce faith," Martin reminds us—*either good or bad*, depending on the words themselves.

The deeper question is this: *What is the root of that thought?* What is it a person truly needs?

If that isn't confronted, then the attitude takes over. Left unchecked, the attitude quietly builds a life disconnected from purpose, from truth, and from God's best.

Sometimes it's downright ridiculous—but sometimes it's sobering, like the true story of a child who ate nothing but french fries until the body gave out. What's consumed—physically and mentally—*matters*. More importantly, what someone doesn't challenge, they silently agree with.

That's why stepping back is so important.

It's the intentional pause to ask:

What do I do really need?

What thought is driving me?

Is this the will of God—or just my habit speaking louder than truth?

Each day holds an invitation to open a mental door. To let light in. To pursue the will of God—even when it means discomfort. Especially when pain opens the door.

Because otherwise, time passes. Not just any time—*wasted time*.

Time that could've been used for healing, growth, movement... or even growing a relationship with the Lord.

Every minute matters. Every word spoken builds a direction of faith—*either good or bad*. That's not just philosophy. It's biblical. It's neurological. It's life-changing.

So talk about it. Reflect on it.

Remember—no one can be everywhere at once.

But they can be present.

His presence is where faith begins.

Reflection Prompt:

Take a moment to step back.

Find a quiet space, free from distraction, and ask yourself honestly:

- What thought patterns have been driving my actions lately?

- Are they rooted in truth or fear? In trust or striving?

- What have I been telling myself I "need"—and is that aligned with what God says I already have?

- Have my habits been forming me into the kind of person I'm called to be?

- Am I allowing space for God to love me... to mature me... to speak to me?

You can ask Him:

"Lord, what do You want me to do today?"

"Where do You want me to go?"

"What thought do You want to plant in me instead?"

Write down whatever comes.

Even if it's one word.

Even if it's silence.

Let that be enough.

Let Him lead the next step.

One thought can change your direction.

One word can shift your life.

Valuable

Trina always sensed that her life was meant to shine. She believed, deeply, that she had been called to be a light—and she lived accordingly. Whether in an office, a customer service role, or a ministry setting, she knew that God placed her in each job with divine purpose. Her assignments were never just tasks—they were invitations to carry light into dark places.

During the 2025 Presidential election, Trina worked in a role that many might have seen as ordinary or temporary. But she didn't see it that way. From the moment she stepped into the building, she had a knowing in her spirit: *God placed me here for something greater.* That conviction was confirmed one night when she noticed a woman nearby wearing a satanic cross. The atmosphere shifted, and so did Trina's posture.

She didn't argue. She didn't panic. She simply prayed.

A quiet, sincere prayer.

Then she looked up toward heaven with peaceful confidence and whispered to the Lord, "I know why I'm here." The next day she noticed that the lady causing stress and confusion with the satanic cross had quit the job.

It wasn't the first time she'd said those words.

Again and again, Trina had found herself in moments like that—moments of alignment, of clarity, of sacred timing. It always confirmed what she already believed:

The Lord never wastes time.

He places His children precisely where they need to be, and He always knows what He's doing.

Before Trina was ever born, God had written her days.

Her assignments. Her intersections with others. Her pauses.

Even her battles.

"Your eyes saw my unformed body;

all the days ordained for me were written in Your book

before one of them came to be." —Psalm 139:16

Trina walked forward in that confidence—not in herself, but in the One who had ordered her steps. She believed that every placement, every delay, every interaction was *ordained*. Not random. Not wasted.

She knew that being valuable wasn't about being busy. It was about being available to God. And when she made herself available, He used her life to reflect His light.

"I am the light of the world. Whoever follows Me will not walk in darkness, but will have the light of life." —John 8:12

"You are the light of the world... Let your light shine before others, so that they may see your good works and give glory to your Father who is in heaven." —*Matthew 5:14, 16*

"We are being transformed into His image from one degree of glory to another..." —2 Corinthians 3:18

Prayer:

Lord, Thank You for being the God who sees the end from the beginning. Thank You for ordaining our steps, even when we don't understand them. Help us to trust that where we are is never wasted when it's in Your hands. Remind us that our time, our choices, and even our delays can be used to reflect Your light.

Teach us to value what You value.

Shape our thoughts, our habits, and our attitudes to align with Your truth.

Let us walk in confidence—not in our own strength, but in Your perfect placement.

Like Trina, may we be aware of our calling to shine.

Let us carry Your presence into every room, every task, every assignment.

We surrender our calendars, our careers, our comfort zones.

Use it all, Lord.

Make us available—and keep us faithful.

In Jesus' name,

Amen.

Our Hearts Intertwined with Him

There is something sacred about putting God first. Not just as a principle, but as a posture of the heart. A daily choice to intertwine one's entire life—flaws, longings, hopes, and disappointments—with Him.

God does not fix His eyes on faults.

He doesn't recoil from weakness or retreat from honest need.

He delights when His children come close—not out of perfection, but out of longing. He loves when they come asking for help. And He answers not with scorn, but with mercy.

Job understood that.

In a world that turned upside down before his eyes, Job still clung to God. When everything crumbled—his health, his wealth, his relationships—he still declared that God was good. That God was just. That God could be trusted.

But the world around him didn't understand.

Even his closest friends tried to convince him to give up hope. To stop believing that God had good plans for him. They mistook suffering for punishment. They couldn't comprehend that someone could be both afflicted and approved by God.

That is the backwards nature of this world.

It mocks those who keep their eyes on heaven in the middle of the storm. It questions the faith of the faithful. But Job's story reminds every believer: God is not finished when life feels broken. In fact, that's often where the real story begins.

For many, the journey feels personal. Just like Job, they may walk through seasons of confusion and waiting. For one woman, singleness became that season. Not as a punishment, but as preparation.

As she walked toward the hope of marriage—a partnership with a man after God's own heart—she became deeply aware of her flaws. Her missteps. Her insecurities. The moments she wanted to rewrite or forget altogether.

It would have been easy to sink into shame. To replay every failure like a film on loop. But instead, something shifted. She began to reflect not on what she had done wrong, but on what God had done right.

She remembered His compassion.

His consistency.

His grace.

He hadn't changed.

He was still calling her to be set apart—for this moment, for this season, for this purpose. She began to see that everything she had walked through had shaped her. It wasn't wasted. It was *appointed*.

"And who knows but that you have come to your royal position for such a time as this?" —Esther 4:14

That verse whispered through her soul like a confirmation.

God had declared her free in Christ. Free from shame. Free from fear. Free from condemnation. He wasn't distant—He was near. And He was making her *triumphant* even in the quiet, even in the waiting.

He was with her in the hard calls, in the days that felt dry, in the moments that didn't make sense. And through it all, she found a friend in Him.

A *faithful* friend.

A *merciful* Savior.

A *present* Father.

She learned that faith was not just believing silently—but speaking boldly. The Word became her foundation, and she declared it back to the darkness.

"Since we have the same spirit of faith, according to what has been written, 'I believed, and so I spoke,' we also believe and so we also speak." —2 Corinthians 4:13

Words held power.

And through those words, her heart intertwined more deeply with the One who had never left her side.

Prayer:

Father God, Thank You for loving so patiently, so completely. Thank You for seeing past flaws and failures and drawing hearts close—again and again. You don't cast away the broken. You mend. You restore. You redeem.

In a world that misunderstands Your ways, help us hold tightly to Your truth. Help us be like Job—faithful when nothing makes sense, loyal when the path is painful, and bold enough to believe You still have good plans for us.

Lord, in the quiet moments of waiting, may we not grow bitter or weary.

In singleness or sorrow, in longing or loneliness—remind us that we are never alone.

You are here. You are near.

And You are preparing something beautiful, even when we can't see it.

We release the shame.

We lay down the doubt.

We silence the voices that say we're not enough—and we choose instead to believe what You say:

That we are chosen.

That we are set apart.

That we are free in Christ Jesus.

Let our hearts be completely Yours.

Intertwined. Anchored. Resting in Your love.

And let our words reflect the faith You've placed in us.

We believe.

And so we speak.

You are God. You know the end from the beginning.

And we trust You.

In Jesus' name,

Amen.

We Can Smell Victory in Faith

1 John 5:4 (NIV) says,

"For everyone born of God overcomes the world. This is the victory that has overcome the world, even our faith."

Victory isn't always loud. Sometimes, it's a whisper in the spirit, a shift in the atmosphere—a scent that something is about to change. Faith senses it before it sees it. Those walking with God often notice it before a breakthrough: a tension in the room, an uneasiness in the spirit, or a missing presence. Something just feels off.

Faith knows when something is lacking. The spirit can detect shortage even before it's visible. The atmosphere may seem "off," and it stinks—not in a physical sense, but in energy. It reveals a need. That's when the believer is invited to step in and infuse the space with faith. To speak life. To carry peace. To bring the power of the Holy Spirit into the moment.

This requires strong core values.

Anyone who has hit a wall spiritually, emotionally, or relationally knows the feeling of being stuck. Sometimes the words spoken don't line up with the fruit being lived. The same power that raised Christ from the dead is available—and that power can heal and restore every part of a person.

One prayer can open the door:

"God, You know everything. You are truth. Please give me an encounter with You so I might know You more—and see the fruit of Your life through mine."

Faith is a process of surrender and healing. God works from the inside out. He restores minds, emotions, bodies, and relationships. Even in areas of life that once felt unmanageable—joy, hope, relationships, purpose—He can and will bring order.

The believer is invited to ask God,

"What would life look like if this part of me were fully surrendered to You?"

That kind of vision brings renewal. Even if trauma or confusion has shaped someone's thoughts or habits, the Word of God matures them. Healing becomes a lifestyle. Growth becomes possible again.

Timing plays a role, too. There's a familiar phrase: *"Timing is everything."* And it's true—even in the smallest decisions. Discernment often shows up in quiet ways, like an inner nudge.

One evening, Trina went to a restaurant during happy hour. The food was familiar and the place was welcoming, but as she sat at the bar, she felt a deep unease. Not fear—just a quiet sense that she didn't belong there in that moment.

Her inner voice said: *"Leave."*

And so she did. She had every reason to stay. She was hungry. The menu looked great. She even connected briefly with someone nearby. But her spirit said otherwise. Trusting that voice wasn't weakness—it was wisdom. And once she left, she didn't regret it. She found something simple and nourishing elsewhere and felt at peace.

That small choice became a reminder:

Discernment is trust in motion.

It's faith responding to what the Holy Spirit whispers—sometimes in places as ordinary as a dinner table.

This is how victory is built—one faithful decision at a time.

Moving on is also part of that faith walk. Letting go of what no longer serves a purpose can be painful, especially if it involves people, memories, or seasons that once brought comfort. But healing doesn't come by clinging—it comes by stepping forward.

Sometimes, what awaits is far better than what was left behind. But the breakthrough only comes after the release.

This doesn't mean dismissing the past. It means learning from it—and moving on with strength and expectation.

Trina experienced this when she began seeking God more intentionally about her future relationships. She longed to be married, but not just to anyone. She wanted a man of God, someone who aligned with her heart and vision. So she began asking for clarity, daily. She invited God into her thoughts, her routines, and her longings.

She didn't want to waste time dating people who weren't aligned with her purpose. She asked for guidance—not out of legalism, but out of wisdom. God began showing her specific things—even the type of man she would be drawn to.

Two months later, she met her boyfriend.

And from the very beginning, it was clear: this connection wasn't random. It was born out of prayer. Out of obedience. Out of trust.

God doesn't bring people together without reason. His plans are always higher. Even when they're challenging, they're for good. He doesn't just arrange relationships—He assigns purpose.

Every encounter is an opportunity to influence culture with kindness, integrity, and light. Like Esther, believers are prepared for such a time as this.

Victory isn't always about loud applause or immediate results.

Sometimes it's sensed.

Sometimes it's quiet.

But it's always real.

Those who trust God deeply begin to smell it in the air—victory, right before it arrives.

The Divine Appointment

There's a truth woven into the fabric of every life: whatever we focus on will grow. When a heart dwells on what is positive, what is redemptive, and what is possible, transformation takes root. Even difficult experiences become teachers. Pain becomes perspective. And in the process, a person becomes *teachable*.

Being teachable isn't about chasing knowledge for the sake of status—it's about staying in a posture of surrender. A posture that says, *"I'm open. I'm willing. I trust there's more to learn."* That posture opens the soul to God's movement.

And with that surrender comes something unexpected: excitement.

To surrender is to trust.

To trust is to grow.

And as one grows, they find themselves increasingly aware of God's fingerprints on everything.

There is, in fact, a divine thread running through each day.

Every encounter.

Every redirection.

Every unexpected moment.

Each one holds purpose—because nothing is accidental in God's economy.

This was something one woman came to understand through a lifetime of seeking, surrendering, and watching God unfold her steps. From a young age, she found herself drawn to silence and stillness. Meditation wasn't a trend for her—it was a lifeline. Her first book, *How Meditation Can Keep You Well*, became the quiet beginning of something greater.

Over time, her practices deepened. She taught yoga to teens with autism, creating a class that combined movement, art, and independence. Using a curriculum called *Not a Box*, she would lead the teens through poses. Each time they followed her lead, they'd earn a coloring page—something they would color, cut, and paste onto a large cardboard box they brought to class. It wasn't just an activity. It was transformation. Growth in motor skills. Growth in confidence. Growth in trust.

That was a divine appointment.

But it wouldn't be the last.

As her journey continued, her heart opened further—to Scripture, to healing, to deeper trust in God's design. She discovered that surrender wasn't a one-time act—it was a *continual decision* to believe that God's plans are more intricate and intentional than any she could make for herself.

The more she let go, the more she saw.

She began to recognize the divine choreography in the people she met, the jobs she was given, even the timing of delays and redirections. Where once she resisted learning, now she craved it. Where once she thought she had to know it all, now she marveled at how much she had yet to understand.

Even her mindset began to shift:

How can I love something I haven't yet learned to appreciate?

Whether it was a piece of fruit, a painting, or a concept in physics, her heart opened in wonder. She realized that everything—even the smallest thing—was calculated with divine precision. Memorizing 45 formulas wasn't pointless. It was part of her assignment. And now, she understood: her entire life was a series of assignments—each one orchestrated by the God who created her with purpose.

Every appointment.

Every pause.

Every person.

Divinely arranged.

Intentionally designed.

Beautifully timed.

That is the nature of a divine appointment. It doesn't always come with fanfare. It often comes quietly—through trust, through a yes, through a decision to keep showing up with an open heart.

When the moment comes—when heaven and earth align in a way that stirs the soul—a person will know.

This wasn't random.

his was God.

Reflection:

Take a moment to pause.

Think back over your life. The moments that seemed small... but later proved meaningful. The encounters that changed your direction. The unexpected detours that led to growth. The people who appeared when you needed clarity, comfort, or challenge.

Ask yourself:

- *What if none of it was coincidence?*
- *What if that job, that delay, that encounter—was by divine design?*
- *What is God trying to teach me through where I am right now?*

What would it look like to live with open hands and a teachable heart?

To surrender your plans not with fear, but with anticipation?

Ask God to show you where He's already working.

Then—watch.

The divine appointment might already be unfolding.

Prayer:

Lord,

Thank You for the beauty of divine timing. Thank You that every detail of our lives is seen, known, and shaped by You.

Teach us to surrender—not just once, but daily.

Make us teachable, open, and eager to grow.

Help us to trust that You are always working, even when we can't see it.

Remind us that no experience is wasted, no meeting is random, and no season is meaningless in Your hands.

You are the Master Designer.

Every moment is purposeful.

Every appointment, divine.

We choose to follow You with faith, wonder, and willingness.

Lead us into what's next—with hearts that are still, listening, and full of trust.

In Jesus' name,

Amen.

In Forever Amazement

So much had happened since that moment—the awkward hug that never landed, the one-sided embrace from a family friend who told her, "Stop everything and move to San Diego." At the time, it felt random, impulsive, maybe even desperate. But that moment became a turning point. One of those divine pivots that shifts the course of a life.

It came on the heels of pain. She had just been let go from a caretaking job—one she took seriously, one where she had done her best. The incident was messy. A wine bottle, left near an elderly woman's medication by an ex-boyfriend. A dinner that felt like a goodbye, though the woman she cared for could barely recall the details. Still, she took full responsibility. Not because it was all her fault, but because that's who she was—accountable, reflective, willing to learn.

And so, when the offer came to start over, she said yes. She packed her dreams, her questions, and her longing for something more—and she moved to San Diego.

At first, she couldn't understand how the city could feel so perfect and so overwhelming at the same time. The beach—*multiple* beaches—stretched endlessly in both directions. The sky painted itself each night in colors no one could replicate. The beauty confused her, stunned her. But deep down, she knew it meant something. It was more than scenery. It was a sign.

Her family friend welcomed her. Her parents provided the plane ticket. And though it seemed like just a change of location, it was far more than that. It was obedience. It was the start of something sacred.

She had always been a dreamer.

Not just in theory, but in writing—carefully, boldly, prayerfully.

She wrote down everything.

Visions for her life, her calling, her relationships, even her impact on the world.

And then, as if confirming that her dreams had been heard, a small thing happened. Her father left a book about San Diego on the coffee table back at home. She didn't think much of it at the time. But now, looking back, she could see it: even then, God had been preparing her for this move.

By the time she was 24, she had seen sunsets over the Pacific that no one could describe. She stood in awe and wonder, time and again. Each evening, the light met the water in a way that made her heart pause. It felt like destiny. It felt like *home.*

She had loved the ocean her entire life. Ask her mother, and she would tell you—her daughter always wanted a house by the beach. Everything about her soul gravitated toward the water. The weather, the palms, the mountains nearby. It all whispered of something ancient and personal. Their roots in Andalucía, Spain only deepened that connection. San Diego felt like a reflection of that lost homeland, but also like the promise of something eternal.

Though her family now lived in West Palm Beach, Florida, and her sister was nearly 3,000 miles away, she had found her place. She knew she had been placed in this city for a reason.

Not just to enjoy the beauty—but to make an imprint.

She saw it everywhere: this world was desperate for love. People were starving for connection but often didn't know how to reach out. Restaurants were filled with patrons looking at their phones, avoiding eye contact, pretending not to need community. But under the surface, they all craved the same thing—to be seen, known, and accepted.

And that's what she carried.

A heart for connection.

A gift for laughter.

A desire to live vulnerably and invite others to do the same.

Because connection doesn't come from perfection.

It comes from presence.

It comes from shared experiences.

It comes when someone chooses to show up fully as they are.

And that's what San Diego had taught her—what God had revealed in those sunsets, those long walks by the ocean, those awkward encounters that became divine appointments.

Every step was leading her somewhere sacred.

Every detail was part of the design.

She now walked in **forever amazement**—

Not because life had been easy,

But because it had been *orchestrated*.

Lord,

Thank You for the beauty You place around us to remind us that You are near. Thank You for the redirections that don't always make sense at first, but later become the clearest signs of Your love.

You saw every moment before it happened.

You led the way with whispers, with sunsets, with unexpected doors.

Help us live in awe of Your timing.

Help us trust that even our missteps are not beyond Your grace.

Let us be present.

Let us be connected.

Let us carry Your love into the places You've planted us.

We stand amazed—not just at what You've done, but at who You are.

And we give You our yes, again.

In Jesus' name,

Amen.

Feelings Change or Chase Us

There's a funny thing about emotions—they either flow with us or follow behind, waiting to confront us later. Some are fleeting, and others linger, quietly shaping thoughts and behaviors. Most people don't realize how often their feelings are directing their choices, until they pause and reflect.

She often thought of that song lyric,

"I am woman, I am fearless, I am faithful, I am divine."

It felt empowering—until the reality of her own internal conflict surfaced. While she considered herself a positive person, she couldn't ignore the quiet current of negative thoughts that still lived beneath the surface. Why? Why did subconscious negativity so often sabotage conscious hope?

She didn't need an answer. She just needed to be honest.

And that honesty became a gateway to transformation.

Instead of ignoring the thoughts or pretending they didn't exist, she started asking better questions. Could she allow herself to *embrace* experiences, even the uncomfortable ones? Could she honor emotions instead of judging them? And could she find the courage to step back from the noise and choose a higher path?

It was the beginning of self-compassion.

Of emotional maturity.

Of learning to listen without reacting.

And she realized something profound:

We all want to be heard.

Not just by others—but by our own hearts.

Intuition, when honored, becomes a compass. It's that subtle nudge that tells a person when something feels right—or when it doesn't. And yet, too often, people override it for comfort, approval, or convenience.

But growth requires a different kind of honesty. It requires stepping out of the familiar.

She learned that conversations—real ones—often begin where comfort ends. When people talk about others or react out of sarcasm, it's usually a sign that they're searching. Searching for connection, for recognition, for resonance. What if those moments could be reframed—not as judgment—but as an invitation to see deeper?

Because when someone chooses to be vulnerable, to speak from their own place of experience instead of projecting onto others, *that's* when growth happens. That's when transcendence begins.

She called it "shedding skin." Letting go of the old ways of thinking and embracing what's newly forming. Her time in San Diego had taught her that. The city itself had become a mirror. The people, the conversations, the stillness—it had all taught her that no one is truly asking about someone else's life when they say, *"Tell me about yourself."*

They're asking, *"Will you be real with me?"*

She learned to speak from where she was. To connect from a place of truth. And in that honesty, she discovered strength. A strength that allowed her to see that *every moment had been building her.* Every uncomfortable conversation, every failed opportunity, every internal battle—it had all played a part.

Even the doors that never opened had served a purpose.

The real battle, she discovered, wasn't in the circumstances—it was in the small daily decisions. To believe or not. To compromise or not. To trust the process, or walk away.

And now, looking back, she saw the beauty in it all.

The setbacks weren't wasted. The delays weren't punishment. They were preparation. And in due season, every promise would unfold.

Not because she had figured it all out, but because she had trusted. She had obeyed the voice of God within her.

She remembered a quote:

"One day you'll look back at all the confusion and realize it all made sense. It was all for a purpose."

That truth settled her soul

She didn't need to understand everything.

She just needed to keep doing the right thing.

Because that builds character. And character builds legacy.

And as she learned to carry that mindset, she also found peace in her body. Grief over lost loved ones had taught her how fragile life can be. She realized that extremes rarely lead to healing. And that forgiveness—especially of self—is a key to freedom.

Freedom to be honest.

Freedom to grow.

Freedom to share her testimony, knowing that someone else needed to hear it.

Because someone out there was struggling too.

Someone needed to be reminded that they weren't alone.

And someone needed to know:

Your story will change lives.

Lord God, You see every hidden thought and every quiet fear. Yet You call us forward—not in timidity, but in boldness. You've placed dreams in our hearts and truth in our bones. Give us the courage to step out in faith, even when the path feels uncertain. Remind us that You go before us, and that nothing is wasted in Your hands.

Let us live with holy confidence—not in ourselves, but in You. Help us trust Your timing, walk in obedience, and speak with clarity and love. May our lives reflect the light of Your presence, and may our testimony be the invitation someone else needs to rise.

In Jesus' name,

Amen.

Purpose

My biggest sense and desire is for everyone to have counterbalancing. What that means is forgiveness with themselves. I just thought of people at bars reading this with a glass of wine saying, "Awareness of personal needs cannot sacrifice our minds. It requires a certain amount of choosing what matters most all the time and giving it more of the time it demands." In other words, we can focus our energies on being intentional to listen to ourselves. Trusting that every experience serves a purpose. We are meant to be loved and give love. To ourselves is most important. If we all took the opportunities after deliberately asking ourselves the question, "What makes the most sense to do?" That would help us get closer to our goals and happiness ultimately.

Boldness with Boundaries

Thank yourself for stepping out boldly.

There was a TED Talk Trina once watched, given by a Canadian woman who claimed she could help people get anything they wanted. At first, it sounded too good to be true—unbelievable, really. But the more she sat with it, the more she saw what Canadian woman meant. It wasn't about control or formulas. It was about *boldness*.

Those who choose boldness—who dare to act, to believe, to step forward in faith—often find more than they expected. Not just opportunities, but clarity. Boldness refines our desires. It helps us ask the right questions: *What do I really want? Why do I want it? How much am I willing to trust God for it?*

Think about those who changed the course of history—Walt Disney, Elon Musk. They saw what didn't yet exist and believed it could. The world said impossible. They said, "Watch me." Where would we be without their courage to build what others couldn't see?

For her, giving her life away to a paycheck was never going to be the answer. she watched her parents build a business from the ground up. Their work ethic was undeniable. But what left the deepest mark on me wasn't just how hard they worked—it was *how they chose to live*.

Her mother especially modeled something different. She prioritized what mattered most. She chose presence over pressure. She stood for her values when it would have been easier to settle. And because of that, our family had options we wouldn't have had otherwise.

She didn't always understand her strength. But now, she sees it clearly. Every day, she faces choices that shape her path. And in those moments, she think of her. Her Mom, thinking of the legacy she created—not just through provision, but through alignment. She taught Trina to trust herself, to trust God, and to never sacrifice what matters most for what seems urgent.

So she thank her. she thanked her father. Thanking them for the foundation they laid. And she thanked *herself*—for choosing to walk it out.

Not perfectly. But boldly.

Because that's how change begins.

But here's the caveat—*boldness alone is not enough.*

The importance of dreaming and achieving one's goals becomes dangerous when it is detached from God, from truth, and from meaningful connection with others.

Trina was moved by the testimony of Katie Anne Phillips, a woman who was swept away during the Texas floods on May 17, 2024. Her heart stopped, and she died—but God brought her back to life. In her supernatural encounter, she stood in the presence of the Lord. In that moment, the truth of heaven was as real to her as the ground we walk on. Her spirit knew she was in a realm of complete peace.

But the Lord showed her something devastating: the condition of America. A shattering revelation. She was sent back not with fear—but with a divine urgency. God instructed her to warn His people: **Do not substitute your time with Me.**

In the vision, she saw Americans across the country glued to their phones. Families were disconnected. Children were being raised by screens. The noise— the constant distractions—were tactics of the enemy. The greatest threat wasn't violence or famine. It was *distraction.*

She saw the power go out. Not for hours, but *weeks.* Darkness came over the Earth. Internet gone. Phones dead. People fighting over scraps of food. Chaos. Silence. Fear.

Her message from the Lord was clear: *Return to Me. Reconnect with each other. Prepare—not with fear, but with faith, humility, and love.*

This reminder is not meant to scare, but to awaken us. Boldness is powerful—but only when it's rooted in Jesus. Dreams matter—but not more than the Dream-Giver. Without Him, we're just chasing noise.

Scripture

"Have I not commanded you? Be strong and courageous. Do not be afraid; do not be discouraged, for the Lord your God will be with you wherever you go."
—Joshua 1:9 (NIV)

Reflection Question

Am I pursuing bold dreams *with* God—or have I allowed distractions to distance me from Him and those I love?

Closing Prayer

Lord, thank You for the strength to step out in boldness. But even more, thank You for calling me back to what matters most—*You*. Keep me rooted in Your presence. Help me discern the difference between forward motion and fruitless distraction. Let me not substitute anything for time with You. Awaken my heart to see what You see.

Thank You for hearing my prayers. Even when I whisper, You respond. Even when I wait, You are working. Strengthen my trust in Your timing, and help me walk each step with faith, humility, and love.

In Jesus' name and through the power of the Holy,

Amen.

Trust

When Trina arrived in San Diego, she came with just one suitcase, $1,000, and a willingness to trust that God would lead her to the right people. What she carried couldn't be measured in possessions. What she brought was hunger—a readiness to grow, change, and become.

Looking back, she could see that everything in her journey required choice. The choice to embrace change. The choice to grow through discomfort. The choice to adapt. The choice to choose God. But perhaps the most important choice was learning to *trust* that the people she needed would find her—and that she would be found.

She didn't move to San Diego planning to stay. It was meant to be just one year. But God had other plans. Even though pain from past abandonment in places like Africa and Europe had left her guarded, He was healing that part of her heart.

In the beginning, she avoided connection. Isolation felt safer. She didn't want to make friends only to lose them again. But over time, something in her shifted. Her heart turned outward. She started to see people. Started to enjoy talking to everyone. What began as survival became *connection*. Relationship. Purpose.

Her greatest transformation didn't come from a classroom or a paycheck—but from embracing what God was doing on the inside.

There had been seasons of change—both *willing* and *unwilling*. But through them all, God was molding her. Her past, marked by the coming and going of people, taught her the value of lasting relationships. Her travels to South Africa and Australia showed her what it meant to form bonds quickly and lose them just as fast. The pain? It lingered. But the purpose? It emerged.

When she arrived in San Diego through the encouragement of a family friend, she had already trained in different speech therapy demographics. She was interested in trauma—helping those who had suffered loss of communication due to injury or war. It was emotionally demanding work, but something about the challenge called to her. It was there, working with people at the edge of their voice, that she started to hear *God's* voice more clearly.

Every interaction became a holy ground for trust.

Still, meeting people had never come easily. She often wrestled with anxiety, with silent questions like *Why me? Why do I have to face these fears?* She wanted others to initiate. She felt she shouldn't have to chase relationships. She came from a family that had always tried to meet her needs—and now, it felt unfair to have to work so hard just to feel connected.

Even her education didn't open doors the way she'd hoped. Instead, she was told again and again: *You're overqualified.* As if her achievements were too much. As if knowing too much disqualified her from belonging.

It was humbling. But it was also holy. Because the real transformation came when she started asking: *How can I trust God if I don't see the way He sees?*

Trust, she learned, required movement. It meant letting go of her own expectations. It meant following those small nudges in her spirit—the ones that called her out of comfort and into obedience. They didn't always make sense, but when she followed them, she began to meet God in ways she never had before.

Prayer

Lord, help us to follow You even when the path feels unclear. Teach us to listen to the quiet nudge of Your Spirit—and to believe that the better You have for us often lives just beyond our comfort zones.

Again and again, God showed up. With perfect living arrangements. With surprising job offers. With peace in places that should've been uncertain. He wasn't just with her—He was *faithful.* And she could no longer deny it: *He could be trusted.*

She began to speak of Him more freely, not just as a distant God, but as a Father. A Father of forgiveness. A Father of love. A Father who invites His children to return to Him over and over, no matter how far they wander.

But there was more. Her story—and ours—is not just about trusting God for personal peace. It's about preparing to *love others well.* The end goal isn't just a blessing. It's becoming a blessing. That only happens when we let go of our self-preservation and live in humility, with open hands and open hearts.

The voice of distraction tries to tell us we don't need more. That we're fine on our own. That we've asked too much already. But the truth is, God wants *more* for us than we want for ourselves. He *wants* us to ask again. To believe again. To hope again.

So Trina began to ask:

- "Do I believe He's truly good?"

- "Has He given me any reason not to trust Him?"
- "Can I still live with personal responsibility while surrendering the outcome to Him?"

Each of us must confront these questions. If we don't, we risk building walls inside ourselves—walls that separate us not just from God, but from each other.

When we allow God's will to shape our lives, something changes. Our decisions begin to align. We become part of a greater story. A story that's not just about *us*, but about *others*. And we can begin to ask not just *what's right for me*—but *how can I reflect God's heart to my neighbor?*

Because if God is good—and He is—then He created us for *unity*. For connection. For peace. Not just inward peace, but *relational* peace.

And this is where the story of Katie Anne Phillips echoes so loudly. When she died in the Texas floods and stood before God, she saw something most of us miss: a nation lost in distraction. Americans glued to screens. Families fractured in the same room. She returned with an urgent message—not to fear, but to *return*. To *prepare our hearts* to live differently.

She saw darkness coming. Power cut off. Phones dead. Weeks without communication. But the greatest loss wasn't material—it was *spiritual*. Disconnection from God. Disconnection from one another.

We must not wait for the lights to go out to reconnect with what matters.

Prayer

Father, prepare our hearts—not just to trust You in the quiet, but to love others in the chaos. Let us see through Your eyes. Let us feel the weight of the world's distractions and still choose to live in peace, in presence, in purpose.

Reflection Question

In what ways have I allowed noise or independence to keep me from loving others well?

Trina knew now: this trust she was learning wasn't just for her. It was preparation—for *loving her neighbor*. For letting others in. For speaking with grace. For listening without hurry. For choosing humility over pride, kindness over fear.

And in that preparation, something beautiful was being born: *harmony*. The kind that only God can create when His children begin to see each other through His eyes.

Dying to Ourselves

There was a point in Trina's journey when she realized that wisdom without self-control would never take her far. It wasn't enough to dream big, speak boldly, or even walk faithfully—she needed to learn the deeper work of *dying to herself*. That inner yielding. That quiet surrender. That unwavering discipline.

She began to see that greatness was never the result of striving alone—but of **faithfulness**.

And faithfulness is quiet. It's strategic. It delays gratification. It plans for things not yet seen.

Trina had to grow in this. She began to apply it in every area of her life: finances, career, relationships. When she desired something big—a trip, a purchase, a vision of the future—she stopped rushing and started *waiting*. Not in passivity, but in prayerful preparation.

She would often think, *Why should I spend what I don't yet have? Why not plan and save, so when the time comes, I can walk in joy, not anxiety?*

She began choosing to pay in peace rather than pressure.

And she noticed the same wisdom applied to her work. When placed in positions where her talents had the chance to shine, she didn't need to prove herself through comparison. Her commitment to excellence—day in and day out—spoke louder than ambition. It spoke of character. And leadership noticed.

Prayer

Lord, teach us the discipline of waiting. Not the kind that grows weary, but the kind that trusts You with the process. Train our hearts to value what's lasting over what's loud.

Trina never saw herself in competition with others. Her only competition was who she had been yesterday. She kept her eyes on what lay ahead—on the inner whisper that more growth was coming. That something greater waited around the bend.

But first, the **dying** had to happen.

The dying to convenience.

The dying to being understood.

The dying to emotional comfort and short-term ease.

Because that's the only way resurrection comes—*when something first dies.*

She started calling it the **Land of Soul Searching**.

It wasn't always a pretty place. But it was sacred.

She walked through deserts—dry places where she questioned everything.

She walked through prairies—those wide open spaces where clarity finally came.

She wandered into tropical lands—where divine connections showed up unexpectedly.

And she bloomed in rose gardens—where her ideas came alive like wildflowers in the sun.

This soul work wasn't about "just being." It was about becoming.

And at the center of it all, was one constant desire: **peace**.

Peace, she discovered, wasn't passive. It was a reward. A fruit of obedience. A gift that came from trusting God enough to let go of control. She began to believe that *peace was the proof*—that she was on the right path.

But peace isn't automatic. It must be guarded. It must be trained for. Peace requires wisdom. Timing. Discernment. And the humility to be *led.*

Prayer

Father, give us ears to hear when it's time to move and when it's time to wait. Let peace rule our hearts—not as a fleeting feeling, but as a confirmation of Your presence.

She remembered what God told her when she first came to California:

"It's the *right choices* that will lead you to live the abundant life I have for you."

That's what it came down to—*choices.*

Choices to be deliberate.

Choices to hold off on temporary pleasure for lasting fruit.

Choices to sacrifice when necessary.

Even something as ordinary as saving for a home became a metaphor. Trina knew that if she wanted something real and lasting, she'd need to make sacrifices. That meant picking up side jobs. Cutting back on expenses. Saying "no" to the temporary thrill of luxury living for the quiet joy of *future ownership*. That kind of vision required more than motivation—it required **tenacity**. Her Pastor at Awaken church in San Diego's voice would recall the latest sermon, " Don't eat your house!"

Because the dream doesn't happen by wishing. It happens by *building*. Letting go of a facade that no one needed to see.

It was in this place of discipline that Trina discovered something deeper.

He sees you.

He is not a distant, angry God.

He is a loving Father.

As she moved about her life, wondering how it was all going to work out, she began to sense a shift. Things around her were *being shaken*. But it wasn't punishment. It was *preparation*.

God was stripping away the things she had unknowingly trusted in—so that her trust would be in *Him alone*.

And if anyone reading this ever wondered whether their prayers mattered—Trina would tell them: *Keep praying.* Even when it feels like nothing is changing.

Even when the answers don't come quickly.

Even when your heart feels dry and tired.

Keep praying. Because your prayers are **weapons**.

Talk to Him. Turn off your TV. Turn off your phone. Silence the noise long enough to *listen*.

Because He's there. He sees you.

He's not punishing you. He's positioning you.

And your job is not to figure it all out—your job is to *trust* and *obey*.

And then—**speak.**

Don't just pray *about* the storm—**declare** what He's already said.

God said, *"Let there be light."* He used His **Word** to *see* and *watch things shift*—more than we realize.

And He invites us to do the same.

Speak His promises.

Declare His truth.

Let your words partner with heaven.

Watch how even your voice, aligned with His, begins to bring light into every dark place.

Prayer

Lord, help us to not just pray—but to speak. To declare. To stand in agreement with what You've already said. Let there be light—in our hearts, our homes, our decisions. Let us speak not fear but faith. Not lack but life. Train our tongues to carry Your truth with power.

Trina knew this kind of dying wasn't the end.

It was the beginning.

It was the pathway to life. Real life. Abundant life.

The kind of life that blooms not from striving—but from *surrender*.

From *discipline*. From *wisdom*. From *trusting the Word—and speaking it boldly*.

What Is the Priority?

At one point in her journey, Trina had to sit down and ask herself a defining question:

What is the priority?

It wasn't a question about goals or ambitions—it was about what reigned in her heart. Because whatever holds first place becomes the anchor of our lives. And if it isn't *God*, then everything else eventually starts to unravel. He will allow a shaking for The Rock to Remain. He is the Rock.

She remembered reading a book called *Get Married, Stay Married* by Pastor Paul Tsika. In it, he wrote honestly about what it means to know your partner's needs—to truly listen, to deliberately communicate desires, and to seek unity early on before differences divide.

In the book, Tsika gave an example: if one person dreams of traveling the world on a boat while the other desires to stay rooted on land, and they never speak about it, that silence becomes a wedge. Needs don't go away; they simply go unmet. And unmet needs often find outlets in distractions, emotional distance, or misalignment.

The same is true in our walk with God.

If we never ask Him to be first... if we never invite Him into our desires, our dreams, our decisions... we'll eventually find ourselves searching elsewhere for what only His love can give.

Prayer

Father, help us to be honest about what we prioritize. Show us what we've put ahead of You, even unknowingly. And give us the courage to reorder our hearts, with You at the center.

Trina had come to learn this firsthand: serving a God who truly *knows* and *cares* for our needs is the safest place to build a life. When God is placed first, everything else starts to fall into divine alignment.

But she also knew it took trust.

And trust takes time, especially when the journey is unclear.

Trina reflected on how people grow in stages. In each new phase, God's presence leads—but only if He is *allowed* to step in. We can do all the right things *for* God and still have a spirit that's dull if we don't spend time *with* Him.

That's where she found herself whispering words from her soul:

"I need Your love. I need it to survive. I need it like I need water. Burn in my heart like a fire. Jesus, draw me closer."

She prayed:

Take me there. I'm going all in. I'm not afraid to get lost in Your love. Show us Your glory.

Because when you have nowhere else to go—you *trust*.

And in that deep place of surrender, something shifts.

The biggest lesson Trina learned?

Don't force anything.

Conversations. Friendships. Relationships. Attention. Love.

Anything forced is not worth holding onto.

If it doesn't flow, let it go.

And in the place of stillness, **discernment** grows.

Discernment is the ability to choose with wisdom, not emotion. The world is not full of truth—it's full of imitation. Without the guidance of the Holy Spirit, people are easily misled by things that feel good but leave the soul empty.

Trina thought of a friend who had once practiced tarot and Reiki. Eventually, that friend realized the subtle counterfeit in those practices—and turned back to the pure truth of Christ. Because truth isn't subjective. Truth is a person. Truth is *Jesus*. And the Holy Spirit leads us in it.

Prayer

Lord, keep us from being deceived by what looks spiritual but isn't from You. Let us be led by Your Spirit and grounded in Your Word. Train our ears to know Your voice—and only Your voice.

People often wonder: *If God is so good, why am I going through so many trials?* But Trina had learned—through sweat and tears and Scripture—that suffering doesn't mean God has left.

She remembered Joseph. Betrayed. Falsely accused. Thrown into prison. Forgotten.

No parents. No inheritance. No visible future.

And still—**he trusted**.

Because *God had a plan.*

As Psalm 34:19 declares:

"Many are the afflictions of the righteous, but the Lord delivers him out of them all."

We are not promised a life without hardship.

We are promised deliverance through it.

In 1 Peter 4:12–13, it says:

"Beloved, do not think it strange concerning the fiery trial which is to try you, as though some strange thing happened to you; but rejoice... that when His glory is revealed, you may also be glad with exceeding joy."

Trina knew—our job isn't to *avoid* the fire. It's to *meet God in the fire.*

The same way He met Shadrach, Meshach, and Abednego. The same way He met her.

We must *never* question God's love based on what didn't happen.

His love is everlasting.

His love *delivers.*

His love turns everything around.

She began to see that faith and love are connected.

"Remembering without ceasing your work of faith, and labor of love, and patience of hope in our Lord Jesus Christ..." —1 Thessalonians 1:3

Trina realized: as her faith grew, so did her love.

And the more she received God's love, the more she could release fear.

So she stopped holding onto burdens.

When she prayed, she *left it.*

She dropped it.

She gave it to God.

Because clinging to stress and fear only choked out her faith.

But *love*?

Love made faith grow without bounds.

Love wasn't just a way to get what she wanted—it was the way to live fully.

To walk bright.

To stay stable.

To carry peace and joy like armor.

And when warfare came—and it did—she was ready.

She knew spiritual warfare wasn't just resisting darkness. It was *advancing in light*.

She was unlocking doors in the spiritual realm that no man could shut.

Doors of peace.

Doors of purpose.

Doors of future promises.

Prayer

Lord, help us to love first. To love deep. And to love loud. Let Your Word be our sword and Your Spirit be our strength. May every prayer we speak be a declaration of trust—and every act of love be warfare that pushes back the darkness.

Trina saw it clearly now:

The real priority isn't just what we *do*.

It's who we put *first*.

And the only priority that can hold up a life is the presence of God.

Serve the Lord with Gladness

Trina learned that the most powerful thing she could do—especially in the middle of uncertainty—was to serve the Lord with *gladness*. Not with heaviness. Not with religious striving. But with *faith*, poured out in gratitude and joy.

What does faith do?

Faith speaks.

As the Scripture says, *"Since we have the same spirit of faith… we also believe and therefore speak"* (2 Corinthians 4:13). Trina began to understand that faith isn't something you merely carry in your heart—it's something you *release* with your mouth. Especially in hardship. Especially when others seem blessed and you're still waiting. That's when faith must become your language.

It takes focus. A little concentration. A heart willing to believe God above everything else.

Trina believed, first and foremost, that God was her healer. Regardless of medical treatments or diagnoses, she trusted in the One who healed every disease in Matthew 8. But she also remembered Matthew 13:58— *"He did not do many mighty works there because of their unbelief."* Faith had to be present for power to flow.

Prayer

Lord, I believe. Help my unbelief. Let faith rise in my spirit—not just for blessings, but for deeper trust in Your love.

Faith without love doesn't last. But when love fuels faith, it becomes a force nothing can stop.

Trina began to speak it aloud:

"I want to release Your Word and take it as my own."

She learned to declare the power of faith:

- Faith receives provision.

- Faith saves from sin.

- Faith frees you from guilt.

- Faith fills with the Holy Spirit.

- Faith pleases God—even in imperfection.

- Faith purifies the heart.

- Faith opens the door to God's presence.

- Faith brings hope, blessing, good works.

- Faith quenches every fiery dart of the enemy.

As Ephesians 6:16 says, *"Above all, take up the shield of faith to quench all the fiery darts of the wicked one."*

But that shield? It only works when *lifted*.

Trina knew that faith required more than belief—it needed **action**. Faith must pray. Faith must say. Faith must respond. As James 1 says, *"Faith without works is dead."*

You can have just enough of God to go to heaven, but never walk in **victory** here on earth. Trina wanted more than survival. She wanted *freedom*. And that meant living by faith as a daily force.

The more she trusted that her sins were truly removed—as far as the east is from the west—the less anything could hold her back.

She began to walk lighter.

She began to walk brighter.

Intrinsically Beautiful

Renewed in faith, Trina began practicing **courage**—the courage to seek God. To know Him. To let Him fight discouragement and unbelief in her mind. She had learned the value of seeking His face. She had learned that His grace doesn't just forgive—it *shields*.

And there was great protection in simply being *still*.

She began setting aside time—just five or ten minutes—to sit in silence. No phone. No noise. Just Him. Because stillness says, *"God, You are first. I need Your voice. I crave it. I make time for it—even when other things feel more urgent."*

As Jeremiah 29:13 promises:

"You will seek Me and find Me when you seek Me with all your heart."

Stillness became sacred. It shifted her lens.

She began to understand that her thoughts weren't always His thoughts, and her ways weren't always His ways. And she needed time to hear *His perspective*—not her own assumptions. Her brain, after all, couldn't process everything. Sometimes, we want to stay positive—but real change doesn't come from pretending. It comes from *truth*. From acknowledging what we believe, finding what's true in it, and letting the Spirit reshape our view.

She learned to change her **perception** to change her **mention**.

To see a different *version* of reality.

To filter life through the lens of *God's voice*, not her circumstances.

Lord, You Are My Hope

Trina often found herself praying from a deep, personal place:

"Gentle Savior, thank You for having mercy on me. You see me for who I really am, and You're relentless in finding me—especially in my most desperate moments. Even when I cannot feel You, I trust that You are the Alpha and Omega. Sovereign. Steady. Good."

She knew now: God had saved her from a life of quiet desperation.

He didn't just rescue her—He *remade* her.

He filled her with peace, wholeness, and a foundation of **His love**.

And because of that, she could step back from fear and choose peace again and again.

There was *no one like Him.*

There was beauty in the process of letting go.

There was transformation in trusting.

Even when life felt like too much, He held the keys—

To her life.

To her freedom.

To abundance in Him.

"Dare to dream," she heard Him whisper.

"For it is the *right choices* you make that will lead you to the *so-called* abundant life I have for you."

She had chosen to serve Him.

And she chose to do it with **gladness**.

A Final Letter to the Reader

Dear Reader,

If you've made it to this page, you didn't just read a book—you walked through a journey. A journey of surrender. A journey of faith. A journey of trusting a God who never stops loving you, pursuing you, and preparing you for more.

Maybe some of these pages hit home. Maybe others stirred questions, tears, or bold new prayers. That's what truth does—it awakens what's already planted inside of us.

Let this be your reminder:

You are seen.

You are known.

You are not forgotten.

The doors you are meant to walk through—*no man can shut*. The battles you face—*you do not face alone*. The peace you long for—*it is already yours in Christ*. And the love you were created for? *It's been chasing you all along.*

Take what God has spoken here and let it take root.

Live it out.

Speak it boldly.

Write the next chapter with your life.

And never, ever stop trusting Him.

With love and expectation, **—Trina**

About the Author

Angie Gomez is a writer, speaker, and faith-filled encourager who lives to see people walk in the fullness of their identity in Christ. After stepping into a season of radical trust, Angie learned what it meant to start over with nothing but a suitcase and a surrendered heart. Her journey—from uncertainty and isolation to spiritual breakthrough—has become the foundation of her message: that God's love is relentless, His timing is perfect, and His purpose for each of us is unshakable. With a deep passion for truth, wisdom, and spiritual growth, Angie writes to awaken hearts, stir courage, and lead others into a deeper relationship with the God who never lets go. Her testimony is rooted in God's promises and the power of prayer. She is deeply grateful to God for the inspiration He's given—and to the friends who asked hard questions about trust, grief, belief, and the hope of finding a Godly spouse.

"We rejoice in our sufferings, knowing that suffering produces endurance, and endurance produces character, and character produces hope."

Romans 5: 3-4